PR FOR
HUMANS

*How business leaders tell
powerful stories*

Mike Sergeant

First published in Great Britain by Practical Inspiration Publishing, 2019

© Mike Sergeant, 2019

The moral rights of the author have been asserted

ISBN 978-1-78860-055-2

Do you want to find a more powerful and authentic business story?

PR for Humans uncovers the essential and timeless principles of leadership communication.

This book shows you how to cut through the confusion and reach audiences with impact – in speeches, presentations, articles, media interviews, videos and podcasts.

We are crying out for more honest and truthful business communication. Delivered by human beings. For human audiences. That's all good PR has ever been. It's all good PR will ever be.

Use these ideas to take control of your business story. Make it more interesting, relevant, personal and valuable.

If you don't, somebody else will tell a bad version of your story for you... or tell theirs instead.

"Mike Sergeant is a PR guru. Brilliant advice on getting your message to the people who need to hear it."
JEREMY BOWEN, MIDDLE EAST EDITOR, BBC NEWS

"The curse of too many organisations – be it in business, government or the law, to name but three – is that they retreat into a private language that acts both as comfort zone and conscious barrier to the access of outsiders. In this stimulating book Mike Sergeant illuminates the self-defeating folly of jargon and preaches eloquently the gospel of plain English."
SIR CHRISTOPHER MEYER, FORMER UK AMBASSADOR TO THE UNITED STATES

"A book that should make the wider PR sector sit up, think, and reassess some of its approaches. Written with real passion, insight and the authenticity of someone who has lived careers on both sides of the camera."
NICK WILLIAMS, MANAGING DIRECTOR, BURSON COHN & WOLFE, LONDON

"Sergeant has got it absolutely right: if you want to influence humans, treat them as humans. Use the words they use and grab their interest through stories."
LORD RICHARD LAYARD, LONDON SCHOOL OF ECONOMICS

"Mike masterfully cuts through corporate smoke and mirrors to provide a wonderfully scripted and hugely credible common-sense guide to public relations, drawing on his wealth of journalistic and PR experience. It nails what is so often overlooked – the power of compelling storytelling and that people are always at the heart of a good story. I'd recommend it to anyone joining the industry."
NICOLA PEARSON, HEAD OF CORPORATE PR, BRITISH AIRWAYS

*"*PR for Humans *is much more than PR for humans. It is an essential insight that can help transform leaders into great leaders. It is a simple masterclass that can help average communicators become great communicators. It shows how to influence reputation through storytelling. This book is a must-read for leaders who want to get to the top, and CEOs or politicians who want to stay at the top."*
EDMUND KING OBE, AA PRESIDENT

"A blast of fresh air. Mike cuts through the nonsense and delivers powerful storytelling lessons in a calm and fluent style. Essential reading."
VAHE VARTANIAN, FOUNDER AND CEO, GLOBAL FAMILY OFFICE COMMUNITY

"Mike Sergeant's brilliant manifesto for PR will help you find the human beings in your world and connect with them through stories they can relate to."
TIM DUNFORD, SENIOR PR MANAGER, USWITCH.COM

"In this age of fake news and failing trust, honest, open PR with the customer at the heart of every message is the only way to progress. Mike's observations and guidance throughout his book are sensitive and thought provoking."
LUCINDA BRUCE-GARDYNE, FOUNDER, GENIUS

"Mike Sergeant has written the ultimate guide on how to effectively communicate. His approach is both genuine and conversational. Guided by his principles and techniques, you will be amazed by how straightforwardly one can transform the way in which they tell their story to the world."
SHK NADIA ALDOSERI, CEO, NDA GLOBAL

"The Mike Sergeant book is a must-read for business leaders in this most challenging time. With a powerful mixture of stories as a journalist to interviewing and working for corporate leaders, Mike underlines the much forgotten 'human' message. PR is about people, it is all it will ever be, if you want to be listened to then tell a compelling story. This book brilliantly tells you how."
NEIL SHERLOCK CBE, FORMER SPECIAL ADVISER TO
DEPUTY PRIME MINISTER NICK CLEGG

"Sergeant is brilliant. A masterclass on ditching the cluttered PowerPoints and alphabet soup of 'PR by jargon', and the importance of authenticity."
GREG ROSEN, PUBLIC POLICY PROFESSIONAL

"For those enlightened leaders who appreciate the importance of building trust, transparency and long-term societal value, PR for Humans is a vital read. It reawakens the need for human stories that engage our emotions and connect us to the underlying ethos of people and organisations. Drawing on his considerable communications experience, Mike shows us how any leader has it within them to use the power of storytelling to lift their organisation towards long-term survival and success."
ALISON SHARPE, ALISON SHARPE CONSULTING

"A small fortune's worth of PR guidance, media and presentation training for the price of a book. And a good read as well."
CHRIS ROBERTS, CEO, INVISION COMMS

"Mike Sergeant brings a welcome fresh perspective and pragmatism to this topic. His advice is engagingly delivered and brought to life with illuminating real-world experiences drawn from his varied careers as a journalist and PR practitioner."

GEORGE EYKYN, CORPORATE AFFAIRS DIRECTOR,
SMART DATA COMMUNICATIONS COMPANY

"Applying filters has become all too easy. Mike's book – drawing on 20 years of frontline experience – is a timely reminder that reality resonates."

LAURA BROOKS, VICE PRESIDENT PUBLIC RELATIONS, MUFG

"Fascinating, fun and full of useful advice."

SIMON LANCASTER, SPEECHWRITER

"A must-read for everyone in business who wants to get their messages across."

SIMON BUCKS, FORMER EXECUTIVE PRODUCER,
SKY BUSINESS NEWS

"Mike is 100% right that getting your story straight is at the heart of effective communication, and his book will help you do that."

GUTO HARRI, COMMUNICATIONS PROFESSIONAL AND
PRESENTER

"A really useful book. In the world of high-speed internet, Instagram, Facebook, LinkedIn, finding the emotional connection with people is more important than ever."

DENYS C. SHORTT OBE, CHAIRMAN AND CHIEF EXECUTIVE,
DCS GROUP (UK) LTD

"Mike has taken the essence of communication from his years as a journalist and now as a consultant and condensed it down to a single message. The power of good story. His book is thus enlightening, practical and informative as well as entertaining. Interestingly enough I observed myself slowing down to read the personal stories as these were the most fascinating aspects of the book. I shall certainly be incorporating these ideas into our future communications strategy as our business is all about human and personal interaction. The numbers are meaningless without the emotional and human connection with our families."

MARK ESTCOURT, FOUNDER AND CEO,
CAVENDISH FAMILY OFFICE

"This book is a great introduction to the art of storytelling and includes many ideas that will help both the professional and those new to the public relations world ensure their story gets the best hearing. Easy and enjoyable to read, Mike draws upon his time as a journalist and a public relations practitioner to give the reader a real insight into how things actually work and how best to get results in the modern-day media."

MARK GLOVER, CHIEF EXECUTIVE,
NEWINGTON COMMUNICATIONS

"A reminder for every PR person to keep it human if you want to keep it successful."

JONATHAN CHARLES, MANAGING DIRECTOR
COMMUNICATIONS, EUROPEAN BANK FOR
RECONSTRUCTION AND DEVELOPMENT (EBRD)

"Every company wants good PR. It's (almost) free and, done well, outperforms advertising every time. The difficulty is that it's harder than ever to get your message heard. PR for Humans *is a road-map for success, and Mike navigates its reader through the pitfalls using the most powerful, and simple, tool available – the story."*

RICHARD SCOTT, EXECUTIVE DIRECTOR OF CORPORATE
AFFAIRS, VIRGIN TRAINS

"Sergeant cuts seamlessly through the chaotic, noisy and sometimes confusing messages widely available to budding storytellers. Clear, logical and beautifully simple, PR for Humans *is the book that other writers wish they wrote."*

PAUL GRIFFIN, DIRECTOR, REPUTATION-INC

"Mike Sergeant is able to talk about PR from the perspective of a practitioner rather than a theoretician. His experience as a senior BBC correspondent enables him to talk about the nuances of PR on the basis of what he has done and seen. His advice comes gilt-edged and is a necessity for those who take PR seriously."

RICHARD MIRON, FOUNDER, EARSHOT STRATEGIES

"Any CEO who wants to master the road to understanding the power behind storytelling, setting clear goals, engaging with staff, connecting with the culture and core values of the company he/she is directing must read this book!"

NEGIN BEMANZADEH, GROUP CHAIRMAN AND CEO,
EEE CORPORATE GROUP

"Whatever your business, if you wish to connect with your audience then I recommend you read this book."

DANNY VASSILIADES, PRINCIPAL, XPS PENSIONS GROUP

ABOUT THE AUTHOR

Mike Sergeant is an international communications coach and PR adviser to CEOs and business leaders. Mike began his career at CNN before moving to Reuters, Sky News and the BBC – where he spent 13 years as a TV and radio correspondent covering business, politics and the Middle East. He then became a director at a leading London financial and corporate PR agency. He now runs his own consulting business.

Mike lives in London with his wife and two sons.

For Georgina

TABLE OF CONTENTS

THIS BOOK

This is not a book designed to criticise the entire public relations industry.

There's good PR and bad PR. Just as there are good stories and bad stories.

I love looking at the world through a positive lens. It's invigorating after many years covering disaster, death and destruction. And yet much of what passes for 'communications' doesn't deliver.

This book is both a manifesto and a guide to something I'm calling *PR for Humans*. This is what it means:

- The most powerful communication is always delivered *by humans, for humans.* We've got to focus on the people who are carrying the messages, and the humans receiving them. Broadcasting 'company news' with no humanity or feel for the audience won't cut it.

- *Story is everything.* For tens of thousands of years, stories have been the main method of moving audiences and shifting opinions. Our brains are hardwired for storytelling. There is no 'PR strategy' without story. Forget the corporate nonsense. Sweep it away and find the story. Facts are important. But stories are vital if you want to enhance reputation.

The principles I outline are essential for those at *all levels* of business, from global CEOs to interns. Whether you're writing documents, giving speeches, chairing events, talking to journalists, making videos, taking photos, hosting meetings or recording podcasts, there are things here I hope will be of interest to you.

I've been on both sides of the fence. As a BBC correspondent, I interviewed presidents, prime ministers and CEOs. Now, as a communications coach, I advise some of the most senior business leaders in the world. Trust me, authentic, powerful stories have financial and editorial value. They can boost careers and lift the trajectory of every venture.

Without good human communication, you can't achieve much in business, or any walk of life. From the most primitive days of our species, stories have been part of every triumph and every disaster. Those with the ability to inform and inspire have changed the fate of nations, and of industries. They've hacked the path of history.

A word of warning: there are quite a few references to long-dead Greeks and Romans in this book. I hope you don't mind. It's partly because my mum is a Classics teacher and partly because I'm married to a Cypriot. But it's also because a lot of this stuff was, of course, figured out in the ancient world.

The essence of humanity hasn't changed. But the world has. And with Artificial Intelligence, technology is accelerating. That's why we need to think harder than ever about what it means to be human.

Do you want to tell a more authentic, robust and powerful story?

Then join me in *PR for Humans*.

www.prforhumans.com

mike@prforhumans.com

If the ideas in this book make sense to you and you'd like to find out how to apply them to your business, then please contact me directly at mike@prforhumans.com

INTRODUCTION

All good stories are human stories. They are about people.

Stories about organisations aren't usually exciting or interesting enough. We want to know about the people leading them. We also want to understand how an organisation affects the lives of real human beings. 'Corporate' or 'government' messages will usually fail to excite or engage people in meaningful ways. Audiences want stories about people.

This is true for governments, corporations, start-ups and charities. They often succeed when a powerful human story can be found and delivered to an audience of humans. They often fail when that story doesn't exist or isn't properly told.

Effective PR connects human leaders with human audiences.

This is what I call *PR for Humans.*

In PR, much then rests on the shoulders of individual leaders. If they can't connect with human audiences in media interviews, speeches, blogs, podcasts, photos and videos, then the 'PR strategy' can quickly unravel.

'Leadership' and 'communication' are inseparable disciplines. Leaders have got to communicate well and with authenticity if they are to succeed.

The way we reach and engage people is with stories. If we are to be good storytellers – and I contend that those in business should try to be – we must be students of humanity, and students of ourselves.

The best stories are within us already. That great speech? It's already inside your mind somewhere. That confident, charismatic media performance? You already have what you need to deliver it. That insightful blog? It's there in your head, or your heart, or your gut already.

So often in communication we look outwards when we might look inwards. We seek to project, when we could instead seek the truth about ourselves and our audiences.

PR for Humans isn't an A–Z manual telling you exactly how to assemble powerful business stories. Storytelling doesn't follow such a prescriptive path. But it is, I hope, a guide and a manifesto, highlighting principles that I think are important. They are:

- Belief – to communicate effectively, you need to believe in something
- Clarity – you must always distil the clearest possible version of your story

- Opinion – to get noticed, you need to have a view and take a position
- Energy – in communication, energy is vital; it's also contagious
- Context – don't just speak about yourself without reference to the world
- Time – leaders must 'own' their past, their present and their future
- Humility – confidence is essential but arrogance is damaging
- Imagery – the best storytelling is visual, even if it only uses words

I'm sorry that these principles don't form a neat acronym or mnemonic in the manner of the self-help genre. Rather than try to crowbar them into such a format, I thought I'd simply share my thoughts and ideas without a rigid and artificial structure. Don't worry about trying to remember them all. Just consider each one in turn. Cherry-pick principles, if you like.

My bigger call to action is a challenge for all of us in the business world to become better human communicators and storytellers. This book is my take on how to approach that. *It's my version of PR.* I hope and expect that your version will differ in many respects. As human beings, the last thing we want is for everyone to be homogenous and predictable.

I look back on my life so far and ask: who have I been drawn to? Who are the interesting leaders and characters?

I like the listeners, the questioners, the humble. I gravitate towards clarity and people who believe in what they're doing. Those with warmth and quiet charm. Those who can light up my imagination and my visual brain, as well as my logical mind. Those who see the bigger picture. Those who can tell me what it all means.

How did I get to this point? Through many moments and many stories. Successes and failures. Twenty plus years of seeing the best and worst of humanity.

I'd like to begin this exploration of communication – and human nature – with two stories from my days as a television reporter for the BBC and Sky News.

Starting in Iraq.

The Awakening – Baghdad, 2008

At a park in central Baghdad two orphans were playing. Both had lost their parents in suicide bombings. One talked openly about his friends and interests. The other was silent. We sat down together on the grass under the heat of the desert sun and began to film a TV interview for my piece on the psychological consequences of the war. I'd already spoken at length to the psychiatrist in Baghdad's main mental health facility, who'd given me a stark warning about the time bomb the country was facing with the exposure of so many children to extreme violence.

I asked the boys about their lives before the bombings, their memories of their parents and what hopes they had for the future. The younger one wouldn't talk at all. I noticed that his hands were shaking.

Back in the edit room at the BBC house in Baghdad, I debated the merits of the story. We had no real 'hard' news. Nobody had produced a credible report on the mental health crisis in Iraq. We had no hard facts or figures. Nobody was launching a major initiative. Nothing had, on this day, changed.

I also wondered whether we could use the 'interview' with the younger boy, as he hadn't said anything. But the close-up shots of his eyes were beautiful and haunting. In the end, we included him and I voiced over the cutaway with the line: "His shaking hands tell their own story".

Our TV report was filed across to London. We fully expected it to be dropped or to be played a couple of times on the little-watched News Channel. In fact, the piece got prominence on the main BBC1 bulletin at 6pm. Then it played again, even more prominently, on the 10pm bulletin. Messages of congratulations flooded in from the programme editor and desk producers in London. The piece was played again and again on BBC World TV and across the corporation's global outlets.

Of all the hundreds of stories I filed from the Middle East, this is the only one that was remembered. The emotional impact of the silent boy was humbling. His eyes and trembling hands captured the pointless trauma of war far better than any number of pictures of guns, soldiers and the aftermath of bombings.

At a time when hundreds of anonymous deaths didn't make news, by focusing on one person we were able briefly to command the attention of millions. In talking to the boy with no parents, I had been thinking like a father. A much deeper, more meaningful channel of communication had been blown open.

The boy was the story.

He was the human being the audience connected with. The story of Iraq was too big for the viewers to take. But they could connect with one person, one human, one child.

I still think about that boy. I didn't use his real name in the report. Now, shamefully, I can't remember it. He'll be a young man now. In my mind, he will always symbolise the terror and hope of Iraq.

Long after I'd left the country, and left journalism altogether, that story stayed with me. But what did I really learn? How did it change me? In what way was it a meaningful part of *my* story?

The violence in Iraq began to ease during a period that came to be known as the Awakening (2007–2009). Sunni tribal leaders rose up and rejected the inhuman fanaticism of Al Qaeda. They wanted a more hopeful and positive story.

American soldiers had been trying to bring stability and progress to the country for years, but they had an abysmal record of doing so. It was only when enough people started to believe in a new story for Iraq – a better future – that the tide began to turn. Just as it has many times during the period of human dominance on Earth.

People make stories. Stories create movements. Movements need leaders.

The Billionaire – London, 2000

Eight years earlier I had another memorable – but very different – television encounter with an individual who has probably touched the life of every person reading this book.

In the year 2000 I was covering some of the craziness that went with the great internet boom. I was working for Sky News as the channel's first (and last!) ecommerce correspondent. It was my job to chart the outrageous successes and the catastrophic failures. I had a lot of fun.

One day I went along to a technology conference in London. The keynote speaker was Steve Ballmer, who was taking over as CEO of Microsoft from Bill Gates. We filmed the event for my piece for *Sky Business Report*. The conference was nearing its end.

The PR officer rushed up and reminded me about another interview I'd agreed to do. Not with Steve Ballmer, the guy I wanted to talk to, but with someone called Jeff Bezos.

Bezos had started a company called Amazon, which was selling books on the internet. It had launched the year before in the UK. I'd never used it. Despite being the Sky ecommerce correspondent, I was a bit sceptical about ordering things online, but I knew Amazon was growing fast – and also losing a lot of money. It was nowhere near profit. Globally, though, Amazon already had revenues of hundreds of millions of dollars. Bezos was, according to the PR brief, already a billionaire, on paper at least.

We set up our equipment. Bezos walked into the room. A funny, nervy man. No great presence. Not much hair – but more hair than he has now.

We had just one camera, and after the interview I needed to shoot my questions from the reverse angle, so we could edit it as a full interview. I made Bezos stay seated while we moved the camera around over his shoulder and filmed my questions again.

He didn't seem to mind. He had this giddy, nervous laugh that erupted from time to time. But when he spoke, he showed some qualities that I now see very clearly.

He had total belief in what he was doing. He understood the context clearly: that the internet was changing everything. He was fixated on getting things right for customers. He was very clear about where he'd come from. He knew where he was *today*, and he had a vision for where he was going.

Plus, there was humility. He spoke about luck. About how he couldn't have started without a loan from his parents. He knew then that it wasn't all down to his own brilliance.

Now, of course, Amazon is worth a hundred times what it was worth on that spring day back in 2000. Bezos himself became, by some measures, the world's richest man. In fact, the richest person ever to have lived.

Quite a story.

Stories Begin – 70,000 Years Ago

When we talk about stories, we're talking about something humans have been obsessing about for tens of thousands of years.

It began with stories. Long before electronic communications. Long before books and printing. Long before symbols, numbers or letters. Long before the first child-like drawings on cave walls. Stories characterised a 'cognitive revolution' that allowed our species to move towards mastery of the planet and supreme technological dominance.

Fire, tools and agriculture were essential steps on the journey to where we are today. But fire and tools were around for hundreds of thousands of years *before* more sophisticated communities emerged. Agriculture is relatively recent and has only been around for about 12,000 years.

Somewhere between fire and agriculture, there was a leap forward that allowed our ancestors to ascend to a position of dominance. Why did they triumph? The persuasive answer given by Yuval Noah Harari in his blockbuster *Sapiens* is that they somehow developed a unique ability that no other species could match: the ability to assemble stories, both fact and fiction.

Other species and early types of 'human' (like Neanderthals and Homo Erectus) had managed to cooperate effectively using simple communication skills, but not among groups of more than about 100. That's thought to be the maximum number of individuals who can connect in meaningful ways with family bonds or shared direct experiences. But imagination brings new, exponentially more powerful possibilities.

Significant numbers of people who are otherwise unconnected can be successfully mobilised into action if they believe in common myths. The large-scale cooperation that was required to hunt more successfully than other human species, and spread cultures over larger geographies, was made possible with stories. As far as we know, Homo Sapiens is unique in this ability.

Storytelling is essential for complex human interaction. Stories weave through every chapter of our civilisation. Their power is as relevant in the modern world of business as it has been for the whole sweep of human history.

The global economy has been shaped by stories, forged by arguments and crafted by the human mind.

Stories Accelerate – Present Day

Now we are living in an age of exciting and terrifying digital acceleration. Stories are created with ferocious speed. They are distributed globally in seconds.

Artificial Intelligence and computer algorithms increasingly determine which stories we see and why. Our human capacity to verify news and information struggles to cope with the chaotic interplay between man and machine. Some 'fake news' is created by bots. But most of the misinformation and misconception propagates through millions of lazy human thumbs on smartphone screens, liking, sharing, favouriting – usually without checking, often without even reading.

As individuals, we can't hope to make sense of all the data. We're just specks in a vast new universe of code. We can't absorb and digest even a tiny fraction of the content. Instead, we dive into obscure rabbit holes, or seek a digital echo chamber to amplify our existing biases and views.

Throughout history, we've looked for mentors and leaders to guide us through the misty swamp. As the algorithms get more powerful, as AI advances, human storytelling becomes more and more important.

Many organisations can spam and share their way to apparent digital prominence. But effective communication comes back to the oldest questions our species has faced: what do we believe? Who do we trust?

Leaders must step out from behind the mountains of spreadsheets and data. They must emerge and rediscover the skill that our species has always had and without which our mastery of Earth would never have happened: *the ability to tell convincing stories and mobilise audiences.*

Stories will help us survive and retain control in the age of super-technology. Robots will never beat us at stories because they can't – and will never – truly understand what it means to be human.

Stories are always about people. Their challenges, their struggles, their mistakes, their hopes and their dreams. They are about how events change characters. How we grow as individuals. How we inspire others to do the same.

Every single one of the 7 billion people on Earth has a story. The starting point in *PR for Humans* is the idea that every one of those stories has value.

My Stories

I have been writing and performing stories all my life.

It started with the plays my brother and I used to put on as children in front of our parents, with detailed scripts, intricate storylines and elaborate staging, in the attic of our West London home.

At school, I was the shy kid in the class. I barely spoke. Talking in front of a group scared me deeply. But, through stories and performance, I gradually found a voice. I also found more and more excitement in overcoming my shyness and being in front of audiences.

As a student actor at Cambridge in the 1990s, I appeared in 16 different productions, playing a range of (mostly Shakespearian) characters, from Claudius in *Hamlet* to Malvolio in *Twelfth Night*. I spent as much time acting as I did studying economics, which I also loved.

This strange combination of theatre and economics set something of a pattern for me. A mix of the hard skills (business and finance) and the soft skills (performance and communication). A blend of the spreadsheet and the story.

When I entered journalism I naturally focused on business storytelling. I loved taking dry subjects and turning them into interesting pieces of television for Reuters, Sky News and the BBC. Then I moved on to political reporting, and then into the dangerous and more colourful realm of the foreign correspondent.

The shyest kid in the class at school had somehow grown into a person who could broadcast live in front of millions of people.

Over 20 years, and in over 20 different countries, I reported the stories of others. Then, in 2014, I moved into the world of business, not as an observer but as an adviser and participant. At first, I found the going hard.

Sometimes the individual *would* have a story, but the business wouldn't. Or there would be a good business story, but the individual couldn't find a personal story to match it. I found the intersection between the personal story and the business story more and more interesting.

I started to make my way in the PR world by sweeping away the leaves and the mud and finding the path. Revealing the story. Getting rid of the processes and structures. Allowing audiences to see the way. Looking for human qualities to follow.

In doing this I grabbed every book I could find on 'leadership' and 'communications' and 'media training' and 'public speaking'. But the real answers only started to come with time, and by taking a deep and honest look at myself – the person I had been, and the human being I was becoming.

What Even Is PR?

Before we go any further, we need to talk about the elephant in the room – the two letters splashed on the front cover of this book. Intriguing us. But also, for some reason, jarring and unsettling us.

PR.

What even is it?

Public relations – or PR – is a misunderstood profession, if it even is a profession. Many people think it is light, insubstantial, manipulative, even dishonest. Think of the phrases: 'That's just PR', 'a PR stunt', 'providing a little PR', 'a PR boost', 'a PR effort to convince'.

To some, PR is almost a term of abuse, aimed at those trying to make the wicked seem wonderful. Ask some people what PR involves and they might say a combination of champagne-fuelled parties and manic political manoeuvring. *Absolutely Fabulous* meets *The Thick of It*.[1]

Even the letters 'PR' have been expunged from the websites of most agencies. Instead of PR, those in the industry prefer (the ugly plural) 'communications' or (even more ugly) 'comms'.

But let's go back to the origins of public relations – *relations with the public*. That's all PR really is: telling people out there what you are up to.

---

[1] Two British TV comedy sitcoms (for international readers unfamiliar with these shows).

Telling your story. And hoping that journalists will recognise it as a truthful, accurate story and pass it on to their readers, listeners and viewers.

This sets up PR against the other disciplines of marketing and advertising. In PR, the theory goes, you *aren't paying* people to give prominence to your story. The story itself must be interesting enough. Advertisers and marketers tend to pay (often huge) sums to newspapers, TV stations, conferences and, increasingly, YouTube and Facebook. In PR, the only money changing hands – again, *in theory* – is fees paid to the storytellers themselves.

The reality is that the waters have got somewhat muddied. The rise of 'marcoms' (uglier still) as a hybrid of PR and marketing means that the old boundaries between 'paid' media and 'earned' media are now very hazy indeed.

On Reputation

This is why many in PR keep coming back to the word 'reputation'. That, in many ways, is the key differentiator. PR is ultimately about reputation. Not directly about selling products or services, but building and protecting reputation.

Your reputation is partly determined by the things you actually do. These are the facts. They are not arguable or debatable. There is no magic PR fix for them. This is real, concrete stuff. If life was a court case, this is where the judgement would always be made: on the facts.

But we also form our views on the stories people tell, and others tell about them.

Reputation = Facts × Stories

If humans were an entirely rational and perfectly informed species, the stories wouldn't matter so much. We would make our judgements about reputation based on a careful analysis of the facts alone.

But humans are lazy and emotional. We are not Homo Economicus (the mythical species in the economics textbooks of the twentieth century that makes its decisions based on perfect calculations using all possible information). We judge quickly, using a few points. We fill in the gaps with story – either the story being told verbally, or a visual one. If there is no story, we'll make one up ourselves.

Facts without stories won't usually build powerful and prominent reputations. Actions without an arc will be hard to evaluate. And if *you* don't tell *your* story, someone else will step in and tell a bad (or untrue) version of it for you.

Some say those in business shouldn't bother with PR. They should just concentrate on making great things, treating people well and leading their companies. But this is to ignore the critical role that stories have always played in reputation.

PR for Humans

Unfortunately, much of the PR industry has lost its way. Yes, there are some excellent practitioners and agencies out there, but there is also plenty of dross. So many of those doing PR don't seem to understand its main purpose: to improve the relations of a business or an individual with the public. To influence reputation through story.

A good story is almost always a human story. *People want to hear stories about people.* And yet PR people are typically hired to boost the reputation of a *company* or an *organisation*. This is where the problems usually begin.

The stories of companies need to merge with human stories if they are to be effective. So the stories of Apple and Steve Jobs became inseparable. Elon Musk and Tesla. For good or ill.

You may also need to find human interest stories within companies that human audiences might be interested in.

"But," say some of my clients, "we are in banking/consultancy/accounts. There aren't any human stories! Only spreadsheets and processes and grids."

"Wrong," I say.

There are always human stories. Your banking activities might be financing infrastructure or renewable energy projects which will be used by people. Your consultancy might be helping the healthcare sector devise better treatments for people. Your accountancy systems might be helping small business owners concentrate on their own employees or customers.

There's always a human story if you know where to look. *PR for Humans* is the search for those stories and the handbook for the people delivering them.

The story is right at the heart of any decent PR strategy. Without a clear human story, the other elements won't be very effective. This is what PR 'strategy' should mean:

1. Objective – knowing what you want to achieve and why
2. Audience – knowing your audience and what you want them to think, feel and do

3. Story – crafting a story that engages them and changes their attitude in some way
4. Tactics – choosing the different ways to get your story out there (e.g. media, social media, speeches, videos, podcasts, photography)
5. Measurement – finding some way to assess the impact of your activity against your original objective

The first half of the book sets out the principles – the things you need to think about to increase the power of your communication. These principles sit right at the intersection of the areas often described as 'leadership' and 'comms'. They are inseparable, for this is the place where PR is at its most useful and compelling.

Each chapter will discuss one of the eight principles in detail. To repeat them:

- Belief – to communicate effectively, you need to believe in something
- Clarity – you must always distil the clearest possible version of your story
- Opinion – to get noticed, you need to have a view and take a position
- Energy – in communication, energy is vital; it's also contagious
- Context – don't just speak about yourself without reference to the world
- Time – leaders must 'own' their past, their present and their future
- Humility – confidence is essential but arrogance is damaging
- Imagery – the best storytelling is visual, even if it only uses words

In the second half of this book, things get more practical. I'll go through the moments of significant extra pressure (e.g. speeches, panels, media interviews, videos, podcasts) when business leaders need to communicate with different audiences in highly visible and sometimes exposed situations.

At each stage, I'll show you how to apply the principles from Part 1 to the real situations you may find yourself in. Throughout the book I will draw on examples and insights gleaned from over 20 years in journalism and business. Each chapter will finish with a summary of the key pieces of advice.

Here's one guiding thought to hold onto: *the audience is everything, but to reach them we need to look inside ourselves.*

The goal is always to move the audience from one point to another. To inform them, persuade them, inspire them. It's always about shifting them somewhere. To do it we must find a beautiful, clear story arc that takes them where they need to go. The best way to do that is to make our communication personal and human.

All too often, those in business dart off in lots of different directions. The trajectory isn't clear. The target destination is unknown. It's a mess. The audience can't be moved because the speaker doesn't know where they're going.

Know who you want to reach and why. Think how you can demonstrate your *humanity* to them.

Understand the audience as humans. Empathise, if you can. Your stories are a gift to them. A precious and valuable gift.

PART 1
Finding Your Story
Principles

1. BELIEF

In this chapter, I introduce the first principle of PR for Humans: BELIEF.
I emphasise the importance of passion and really understanding why your
organisation does what it does.

Believe in Something

The most useful question to ask yourself in business is: what do I believe in?
People who *care about something* are the ones who cut through the noise and
enhance their reputation. They are the masters of *PR for Humans*.

Find something to believe in. And stick to it.

This is sometimes dressed up as the corporate 'mission statement' or the
'purpose' of a business, implying that there needs to be wider relevance and
social benefit. Good for profit *and* good for the world! It might be, but it
doesn't have to be.

The problem with the word 'purpose' is that it's been used to justify the
way some organisations make huge sums of money. They've carried on with
business as usual *over here*, while launching schemes *over there* to show they
have a conscience and aren't destroying humanity or the planet. Many seem
to think business purpose means things like cutting carbon emissions, saving
rainforests or fighting obesity.

I don't want to be glib about this, because those who care about charity
and have a real connection to the world are already the heroes of *PR for
Humans*. But the focus on social responsibility has confused and muddled
one of the most important principles of communication:

You must believe in what you are doing. It must have intense meaning for
you.

It's about passion. To be a convincing communicator, it's got to matter
to you. Not to your stakeholders or lobbyists or friends. To you.

You might be running a clean energy business. Or you might be looking
after the wealth of the world's billionaires. You might be making healthy salads
or constructing high-speed rail lines. Some people may love what you do. Some
may not. But only you can ascribe meaning and passion to your activities.

No clever argument or positioning or reasoning will win if the audience senses that the belief is missing. This is the first principle of *PR for Humans*.

Companies don't care about anything. They are legal constructs, not living beings. Organisations don't have emotions. It's the people within those organisations who feel things. And the customers who buy their products.

In business, you need to show the world what *you* care about.

Here's an example from my *PR for Humans* podcast. Lucinda Bruce-Gardyne is the founder of Genius, the gluten-free bread and baking products company. She set the company up 10 years ago after discovering that her son was severely gluten intolerant. He was three years old and tiny. He'd been feeling sick off and on since he'd been weaned.

Once the diagnosis came through and gluten was removed, he was a changed child. Within two months he was running around. But Lucinda couldn't find a decent loaf of gluten-free bread to make him a sandwich. She was a trained chef and a food expert, so she set about solving the problem herself, like a woman possessed. Obsessively blending ingredients in her kitchen. Baking 14 loaves a day. Working night shifts in a bread factory nearby to try and scale the recipes. Looking after the kids during the day. Desperately trying to get the formula right for a viable business to scale up.

"I was on a mission," she told me. "I don't think I could have got as passionate about a chocolate cake. I was driven by the need to sort the problem out. My primary motivation was my family. My secondary motivation was I knew I'd spotted a gap in the market. I could see this was a way of making a huge difference to people."

The drive. The passion. As Lucinda told me this, her eyes were shining with the authentic belief. She was someone who knew exactly what she'd done and why she'd done it. The story rang true.

Today, Genius exports to 10 countries, employs 300 people and has a turnover of £30 million.

Just to emphasise, this is about *your* belief. What *you* care about. Not adopting somebody else's values and expectations.

Your belief might be in gluten-free, healthy products or fantastic takeaway pizza. It could be electric cars or powerful 4x4s. Other people will make their judgements. But from a communications perspective, it's what *you* believe that matters.

In another example, the CEO of McDonalds, Steve Easterbrook, did an interview with the *Sunday Times*. Of course, he was asked about obesity and healthy eating. He told the reporter not to "hold your breath" that the fast food company would be "building the menu" around kale and salads.

"If you can have a hotter, fresher and tastier burger and hot fries, that's how you're going to satisfy the majority of people," said Easterbrook.[2]

Hotter. Fresher. Tastier. Burgers and fries. That is what Easterbrook was passionate about delivering for his customers. You may disagree with the statement. You may think McDonalds should be doing something else. But it struck me as being very authentic. After reading it, I have personally visited McDonalds more frequently. When I do, I think, *the CEO of this place cares about hot, fresh, tasty food.*

I can't tell you what to care about. You've got to figure that out for yourself. I'll give you one clue, though – it can't just be money. You need to believe in something else. Once you do, your speeches, media interviews and articles will be a lot more powerful and convincing.

Passion is also contagious. If you really feel it – and indulge it – others will too.

As the American writer Ralph Waldo Emerson once remarked, "Nothing great has ever been achieved without enthusiasm."

Be a Hedgehog

Your beliefs and passions don't have to be dazzling. They can be routine. Some may even consider them boring. That doesn't matter. If they drive you, they will be effective.

In business, as in life, natural talent is delightful. But it's nothing compared to relentless determination. That is the quality I've seen in all the great leaders I've interviewed and worked with.

Excellence is a habit, as Aristotle taught. If you can demonstrate personal consistency across your professional life, you will send the most powerful reputational signals. If there is a secret sauce for leadership communication, this is it. Consistency wins trust, and trust brings respect.

This is how Hazel Moore OBE, the chair of international investment bank FirstCapital, put it in the conversation we had on the *PR for Humans* podcast:

---

[2] Sunday Times newspaper interview, 7 January 2018, 'The Wizard from Watford Shaking up McDonalds': www.thetimes.co.uk/article/steve-easterbrook-the-wizard-from-watford-shaking-up-mcdonalds-qjkv6r8ll

[As an entrepreneur] there's definitely that element of drive and passion and resilience because there are always knock-backs. But it's also vital to be able to communicate an idea and a vision. Because you are always selling. You are selling to potential employees. You are selling to investors. You are selling to customers. And you may not yet even have a product. That ability to communicate is very important for entrepreneurs.

In his celebrated management book *Good to Great*, Jim Collins identifies the central quality that turns a good company into a great company: having a 'hedgehog' approach. The foxes of business may be darting after every new fad and commercial possibility, but hedgehogs slow things down. They keep moving. They simplify a complex world into a single unifying idea, a basic principle or concept that frames everything and guides progress. They keep going at it. In the long run, hedgehog companies are the ones that, according to Collins, make the leap to greatness and stay there.

Hedgehogs develop the habit of consistent excellence.

It turns out, having a jumpy, 'commercial' mindset is – aside from annoying – happily not the route to lasting success. It is a rather tense and nervy way to drive performance in the short term. Chasing cash, fighting for fees, gunning for growth, pushing for profit, running after revenue – these are all ways to build unhappy and ultimately unsuccessful companies. Managers will be disliked. Employees will burn out. Customers and clients will grow suspicious. Reputation will ultimately suffer. Journalists won't like talking to you.

One of the biggest, most pleasurable surprises on crossing from the BBC into the private sector was discovering how helpful so many people are in the supposedly cutthroat world of the free market. In business, those who are overtly commercial at the expense of others quickly find they lose the most important commodity in the market: trust. Without it, you can't operate.

The best way to be trusted is, I believe, to be completely clear about why you are doing what you are doing. If you can display your own sense of value and demonstrate what really matters to you, others will follow. At some level, this is usually about helping people, whether they are customers, clients, investors or employees. Helping them do something, or achieve something, or have something. It doesn't have to be altruistic. It just means finding a way of using your skills and abilities to serve other human beings. The money may then follow.

Connect

In serving people, we need to find ways to connect with them. The old economic models based on price and information have been challenged in recent years by new models of influence and behaviour. The bonds with our audiences have never been more important. The aim for any business leader is not to sell *to* people but to connect *with* them. That's where real economic power is now generated.

The need for companies and individuals to connect with audiences and to demonstrate the point of their existence is brought to life by former BP chief executive Lord Browne, in his book *Connect*. Browne is (rightly) dismissive of certain types of PR that promise to 'manage' reputation and spin elaborate, fictitious webs. He describes reputation as an outcome of everything that a business does. It's a function of all the company's products and activities. It is about connecting with people as you really are, not as you would like to be.

As Socrates said, to gain a good reputation you must endeavour to "be what you desire to appear".

Reputation is, argues Browne, a reservoir of goodwill that must be filled up over time from many deep, authentic sources, not artificially engineered for short-term gain or quick recovery from a crisis. Listening to the former BP boss, you might believe there's no role at all any more for the storytellers themselves. All a company should do is be authentic. Do everything as well as you possibly can, all the time, with a simple unifying idea, and reputation will be assured.

"But," I asked Lord Browne, at an event I chaired at the Royal Institution, "when it comes to telling their stories in interesting ways, don't even the best companies need a little *advice*? From time to time?"

Browne turned to me with a broad smile. "Only... from certain individuals!" he said, patting me on the shoulder with a sideways glance at the assembled crowd of corporate affairs and PR advisers, who had feared being written out of existence with a single answer. Laughter and relieved applause erupted in the hall.

Your actions are important, for sure. But so too are your stories. Reputation requires both. To connect with its audiences and the world, every business leader needs to have a 'why'.

Apple is the company that is most often given as the defining example of a company with a clear 'why'. As Simon Sinek said in his blockbuster

TED talk,[3] Apple was wildly successful not because it set out to make great computers, but because Steve Jobs came up with a clear sense of *why* it existed. According to Sinek, Apple's mission was to challenge the status quo and make beautifully designed products that changed the world. That doesn't mean that Apple set out to 'do good', necessarily. But it had a clear and – for its users – very meaningful story. It had a 'why', and that meant it could connect.

Note also that Apple took over the world by getting *other people* to tell its stories. Famously, the company didn't often engage directly with journalists and media. Apple didn't do conventional PR. Apple didn't really do its own proactive social media at all, either. Instead, it built an energised base of fanatical tech fans who packed out every product launch and swamped the internet with Apple love at every opportunity. Apple was the near-perfect example of defining the story and getting other people to go out and tell it – to evangelise for the company day after day, month after month, year after year.

Arch-rival Microsoft was watching and learning (slowly) all the time. In his book *Hit Refresh*, Microsoft CEO, Satya Nadella, describes how he had to redefine the culture within Microsoft, refresh everything after the long years of control by Bill Gates and Steve Ballmer. Nadella says that Microsoft needed to rediscover its soul. Employees and customers didn't really understand why Microsoft existed any more. They needed a new, better story.

Nadella describes how he set about refreshing the culture and putting new meaning into Microsoft. Everyone in the company had become a bit of a know-it-all, out to prove they were the smartest in the business, score points and, unwittingly, stifle creativity. Ideas were getting lost in the hierarchy. The customers were 'outside' the business. They were just the people who eventually happened to buy the products. Nadella put customers back at the heart of Microsoft and made it clear that everything the company did had to be consistent with one big idea: helping people around the world to lead more productive lives. It was essential for the business to reflect the diversity of its millions of customers.

The story was now better. There was a central belief. The customers started to get it. The business was connecting again. And, yes, the share price rose.

There was much more CLARITY – and that is where we are heading next.

---

[3] Simon Sinek, TED talk, 'How Great Leaders Inspire Action'.

Summary

- **Believe in something:** As a leader, you need to show the world what you care the most about. Not money, but something else. A desire that makes you human.

- **Have passion:** You need to build your communication around the thing you're most passionate about. It may be good for society. But it doesn't have to be. The important thing is that it has intense meaning *for you*. That is *PR for Humans*.

- **Be relentlessly excellent:** Keep showing up. Become dogged in your pursuit of excellence. Be known for doing something superbly well *for other people*. That's how to connect.

- **Understand why:** Discover (or rediscover) why you do what you do, why it matters and to whom. 'Why' is the best human question.

2. CLARITY

This chapter focuses on CLARITY and the importance of finding a single headline for each moment or event. I also discuss the need to 'soar and dive' between specific examples and the big picture.

Seek Clarity

The best communication is like the purest mountain stream. The water is loaded with nutrients and salts, and is perfectly clear.

Poor communication is the polluted and muddy, slow-moving river. The water is toxic and impossible to see through.

Clarity.

Clarity is what we seek in *PR for Humans*. In communication, clarity is one of the highest virtues.

Clarity is related to, but not identical to, another quality: simplicity. I was once taught that the two stages of putting together a broadcast news report are:

1. Decide what to leave out
2. Decide what else to leave out

With each iteration, we get to a simpler version of the story. But as time has gone by, I've started to question this a little. Stripping away layers usually gets you to a better place in communication, but now I think simplicity can't be the destination. The final goal must be clarity.

Clarity is beautiful and flawless. Simplicity can lack sophistication. If we keep taking things away, we may ultimately arrive at something facile. This is the old problem of 'dumbing down'. Make it simpler and simpler and simpler... until it is simply vapid.

If we start with 100 slides, each containing five bullet points, we can make things simpler by cutting back to 20 slides with three points on each. Sure, it's an easier watch, but we may still be a long way from having a clear story.

Seeking clarity is the act of purification and distillation. We are not always trying to make the complex simple, but to make it *lucid*. The issues, ideas and arguments we tackle can still be elaborate and intricate. With storytelling, there is beauty in clarity, even if some of the themes we speak about are the most challenging and complex subjects in the world.

To go back to our polluted river. We can remove millions of gallons of water until we are down to one last murky glass. This is a much simpler situation, but we still haven't achieved real clarity. The next time a CEO, business leader or politician comes on the TV or radio, ask yourself: is this a glass of mountain water or a mug of indigestible sludge?

How do we achieve clarity? Ah, that is the million-dollar question. If you can find real clarity, I'd wager it would be worth at least a million dollars to your business. I think it's partly a question of getting the right sequence in place for solving the problem.

If, for instance, we start with a huge pile of documents and then try to turn these into a speech or a communications plan, we're unlikely to find clarity. We are approaching the problem the wrong way around.

We should be imagining our audience first, asking ourselves: what do they know about us? Think about us? And what would we like them to think, feel and do? If we had to walk onto a stage and had just 10 seconds to tell them something about our organisation, what would we say? Can we straighten this story out in a way that's meaningful for us and for them?

We're not just seeking a one-off slogan or a soundbite. We're trying to find the source of the crystal-clear stream that can take us all the way to the ocean.

One source of clarity is to apply all your focus, at any moment in time, to one thing.

Fire One Arrow

In the fantasy action show *Arrow*, the hero sometimes puts two or even three arrows into his bow at once and shoots multiple baddies standing in different places. This is usually a funny and exciting moment in the episode. But, of course, it is near impossible. Any archer will tell you that you can't fire more than one arrow at once and realistically hope to hit any targets. It's always better to shoot them one at a time.

And so it is with communication. We can't shoot several arrows at once. If we try, they'll either clatter to the ground or flip off into the sky on a random trajectory, missing the audience completely.

Sometimes communicators will talk about the 'rule of three'. The idea is that a list of three things is pleasing and easy to remember, so presenters and PR people will put three headline bullet points on a slide or document. But I think this is often still too confusing.

Newspapers don't have multiple headlines for each story; they have one. The body of the piece can contain much more information and several angles, but the story, on a given day, should have the clarity of a single thought.

I'm amazed that so many press releases sent out by professional communicators contain three or four different 'stories' listed as bullet points at the top of the page. And those are some of the better releases. The worst ones are impenetrable blocks of text and numbers with no clarity at all. Hedging your bets like this shows a lack of confidence about your main story, as if you don't really know what it is. I would advise all businesses – in every piece of communication – to present just one headline.

Shoot one arrow at a time.

When I started out working on the BBC's *World Business Report* in 2001, we would cover the results of the main companies that were reporting on a given day. I would report live from the London Stock Exchange and try to make sense of the financial statements that were pushed out by listed businesses at 7am. These were usually impossible to decipher, unless you were a professional analyst or a complete nerd.

Then one day something radical happened. The editor of the show decided that the BBC would only cover financial results if there was a story. We wouldn't just read out the numbers, lists and key points given to us by each company. We would only report when we were confident that we could write a (single) headline that would be interesting to the viewers. It's a good principle and one that business people should remember.

The power of focusing on one thing at a time is what delivers exponential results, as Gary Keller outlines in his bestselling book *The One Thing*. Find your single idea/priority/headline and everything else fits into place.

This discipline was drilled into me again a few years later in my career, when I was filing dispatches for the morning programmes on BBC Radio 4. As well as writing the body of the piece, I would always write the headline that the announcer or presenter would read out. This was critical – particularly the very first sentence. In news this is often called the 'topline', and it would have to capture – in five seconds – the main point of the story.

Think of the greatest speeches in history. We only remember one line. "I have a dream". "Tear down that wall". "*Ich bin ein Berliner*".

Think of the key moments in politics. There's only really one thing that dominates. Who won the election? What did the minister say? Why did the bill fail? Who resigned? Why did the policy unravel? The headline on a given day is likely to be the answer to one question, not several.

You can't go on stage or into a media interview and try to cover 20 different things. You can't even, I believe, do three things properly at any one time.

No – with apologies to the Green Arrow – you can only shoot one bad guy at a time.

For every moment you need just one arrow.

And, for some people and some businesses, there is only ever one arrow.

If at times we still need to convey more than one thought, idea or piece of information then we must 'soar and dive'.

Soar and Dive

When thinking about your communication, imagine you are flying a chopper. In your helicopter, you can surge upwards into the sky. From thousands of feet up, you can see the big picture. In communication, this is your big-horizon stuff.

You can hover above a certain point to see what's in that area, and you can land where you choose. The specific landing sites are your examples. These are the moments when your communication becomes really detailed and really targeted. You might mention an exact location, reference a certain company or name individuals. These are the case studies that allow you to illustrate the bigger ideas and issues.

As a CEO, you need to fly your metaphorical chopper around the city, observing the skyline from up high and then touching down at the very specific points you want to visit.

Soar and dive.

I learnt this as a television reporter. On the day I was heading off to cover the Boxing Day tsunami, I was a bit nervous about how my reporting would match up to the enormity of what had happened. When 200,000 people had died, how could I hope to convey the scale and full impact of the devastation?

The editor of *BBC Breakfast* took me to one side. "Focus on people," was his excellent advice. "Tell the story in *more depth* about one family or one individual."

In other words, use the micro to convey the macro. Focus tightly. Go in deeper. Connect on a more specific, personal level. Then pull out for the 'what does it all mean' stuff (sometimes called WDIAM at the BBC). Dive in. Then soar.

I used this technique for the next decade of my TV reporting career.

So, if I was telling a story about, say, refugees in Lebanon, I would focus very tightly on one family. Build their story. Allow the viewers to get to know them a bit. Then – perhaps in a piece to camera – I would soar up and out for the political and regional perspectives. Then fly back down into the specifics, maybe with the same family, maybe with another very focused and specific example.

If I was doing a story about the government's benefit changes, I would find a family affected by them. Tell their story. Then soar out to Westminster for the big-picture policy debate. Then back to the family.

Soar. Then dive. Then soar. Then dive. Macro to micro. To macro. To micro. Big picture to human interest. To big picture. Back to human interest.

Some people get stuck because they focus on examples and lists and meetings, without ever flying their choppers up to 10,000 feet for the high-level, long-range view.

Some people get stuck because they fly too high. All sweeping analysis. No specifics. No attention to the human detail. Never seeing things up close and personal.

The human beings at the centre of the story – whether there are 10 of them or 10 million – must get the focus they deserve. You don't want to fly your chopper way up high so you can't ever see them close up. You need to touch down regularly, talk to people... and sometimes invite them up for a ride.

Find clarity by soaring and diving.

Your examples often need to be tied together with an OPINION. That's the next stage of *PR for Humans*.

Summary

- **Seek clarity:** Even if the subject is complex, you can always distil it. Find the clear thread that runs through the story. Clarity is related to simplicity, but they are not the same. Humans love clarity.

- **Find one headline:** Don't try to tell a story with three or 10 headlines. Your speech, article, video (or anything else) should have one clear headline that captures the story. Humans want to focus on one thing at a time.

- **Soar and dive:** Find the combination of big-horizon storytelling and specific examples. Don't always go macro or always go micro. Clarity comes from the combination of the generic and the specific. The human stories *and* the grand ideas.

3. OPINION

This chapter looks at the importance of having an OPINION in business. It doesn't have to be political or controversial, but those wanting profile and reputation mustn't simply list things – they need to interpret the world.

Take a View

Presenting tedious facts and figures. Going through boring agendas. Listing meaningless achievements and projects. Sound familiar? Yes, this is what most business 'communication' sadly consists of.

Those wanting to do *PR for Humans* must do something else. They must tell the audience what it all means. They need to convey an *opinion*. They've got to stand up on the stage and express a view.

This may seem strange coming from someone who has spent most of his career not taking sides and not having opinions (or at least not ones that could be publicly revealed). At the BBC my reporting had to be strictly impartial. But opinions are the currency of leadership communications. They get you quoted. They show a decisive mindset. In a confusing world, they are the best way of showing that you are the person who can make sense of it all.

As a reporter, the big red line was expressing a party-political opinion. Sexism, racism, homophobia and other forms of discriminatory opinion were also, thankfully, completely out – as they should be in any organisation and walk of life.

As correspondents, we were supposed to say interesting things and analyse the situation, without ever piping up too strongly for anything. This was a hard balancing act much of the time. The toughest situation was probably reporting the Israeli–Palestinian conflict. The BBC was always under fire from one side or both. I made sure I chose my words with immense care when doing live two-ways from the TV studio in Jerusalem with the presenter in London.

Interestingly, when I caught up with the BBC's Middle East editor, Jeremy Bowen, years later for a chat in front of the fire at his London home, to record an episode of the *PR for Humans* podcast, I put this idea to him:

that BBC correspondents always had to be 'on the one hand this, on the other hand that' people.

"I don't do 'on the one hand, on the other hand'," he shot back, fielding what must have been a familiar challenge. "My job is to tell the truth as I see it."

Perhaps from the lofty vantage point of one of the BBC's international editors, the 'truth' is an easy thing to see. Bowen's years of experience and mastery of the Middle East may allow him to cut through some of the restrictions. I never felt I had licence to do that. My reporting had to be balanced to the nearest microgram.

One of the hardest transitions in moving from journalism to public relations and communications is the need, suddenly, to take sides. You have a client. They have a position. You need to find their story. A big part of that is working out their opinion. This may be slightly different from your opinion, which is OK. It can't, though, be the complete opposite. Some PR people act like lawyers, going into action for heroes and villains with equal gusto. I could never be one of them. The best PR people, I believe, choose their clients within some sort of moral framework.

I feel a certain empathy for business leaders, whose every word is analysed for signs of bias. I'm not surprised that many are nervous about standing up and standing out from the crowd. But if they want to cut through, they do need to plant their flag somewhere.

In their book *The CEO Next Door*, Elena Botelho and Kim Powell identify decisiveness as one of the four key behaviours of successful business leaders. It may sound obvious, but their rigorous research is impressive, drawing on a study of the performance of 2,600 leaders. Decisive CEOs are 12 times more likely to be high performers. Whereas most of the decisions CEOs make will happen behind closed doors, the biggest ones will attract public scrutiny. At this moment the audience is asking not just what the person has done, but why they've done it. The CEO's ability to hold and defend a properly thought through opinion appears to be critical.

The opinions held by business people are occasionally political and controversial. But most of the time they are not.

In recent years, businesses have moved further back from political involvement. Because their audiences are diverse and digitally active, businesses are much more careful than they used to be about their own activism. If they're seen to be shoving an agenda down the throats of their customers, they risk losing them quickly. Now most CEOs and consumer-facing organisations keep their heads down and stay as neutral as they can on social and political issues, unless there's an easy win to be had from backing a campaign against an obvious menace.

One clear illustration of this could be seen in the difference between the UK's first EU referendum in 1975 and the Brexit vote of 2016. In the first popular vote, businesses were active campaigners; even the big supermarkets backed the 'yes' campaign. But 41 years later, businesses had lost their stomach for the political fight. The main industry bodies – like the CBI (Confederation of British Industry) – of course supported the 'remain' camp. The number of CEOs who came out strongly for one side or the other, however, was a tiny percentage of the total.

So if they can't easily have social or political opinions, what should business leaders take a view on?

The safest areas are: market trends, consumer trends, economic changes, technology shifts and diversity. These are the slam-dunk topics that CEOs and board-level executives should craft a position on.

Stop Being the Accountant

OK, so the territory has been identified. But how do you then work out your position? To some, it comes as naturally as breathing. To others, it's easier to walk 500 miles than to come out with a crystal-clear view.

The difficulty comes when the CEO or spokesperson hasn't come up through the corporate affairs or communications route. Perhaps they were the chief financial officer or chief operating officer in their previous role. They know every part of the company like the best engineer knows their machine. But when asked to look *outside* the business at the big world, they can easily falter.

But find a broader set of views they must, if they want to be noticed.

Every morning, as I prepare for media training sessions with bankers or professional services experts, I look through the *Financial Times* and circle the quotes. I'm asking all the time: who is getting quoted and why? If a journalist is sitting down with someone for 30 minutes or even an hour, which 15–20 words are they sniping and inserting into their article?

The simple answer is this: it's *opinions* that get quoted. Not numbers or facts. Journalists do not quote information. If it's useful, they will insert relevant facts in the rest of their story, but they will *quote* the bit where someone gives their view on what it all means and why it matters.

Understanding this is of supreme importance for anyone in business wanting to improve their communication skills. Sure, present 20 PowerPoint slides to me with heaps of evidence and exhaustive analysis, but be prepared for the challenges:

"Yes, but what does it mean?"

"What does this tell us about the world?"

"What, in your opinion, should happen because of this?"

These surprisingly straightforward questions can wrong-foot even the most experienced senior partner or board-level executive. They will often give a rambling answer, talking about whatever their management preoccupations are at that precise moment.

But if you are the leader, you need a clear view of the land ahead. You can't lead if you can't decide where to go. You won't be able to decide without an opinion on the *future* (about which more later).

Watch Your Personal Space

Sometimes those in business will preface their answer to a question in a media interview with, "My personal view is...".

Their hope is that, somehow, by making it clear that these are *their* opinions rather than official company policy, their audiences will allow them more freedom. This can work in certain circumstances, when the person has a clear public identity, social media profile and presence that is distinguishable from that of their company.

Unfortunately, the 'personal view' is a risky path to go down for most spokespeople and business leaders. The journalists and others in the audience will not usually distinguish between the views of the individual and the position of the company. If you are representing a bank, an insurance company or a professional services firm and you articulate *your* view, the reporter will likely just quote you as "X from Y said Z". The personal view and the business view are soldered together. Then you will have to explain to the board why you've made up a new policy live on air...

I'm not saying you can't have a personal view. You must. But don't expect the outside world to differentiate the personal opinion from the view of the business.

When I was at the BBC, for 13 years my personal views had to stay firmly within the confines of my family and circle of friends, and even then I would feel nervous about coming out with strong statements on one thing or another. A career of seeing (at least) two sides to every story makes you naturally suspicious of those with huge levels of political certainty. The more I look at the world, the more complicated it becomes. The harder it is to be sure about anything. But you must take a view.

You need to have joined the dots in the right way. You must show the decisiveness of opinion that gives you the confidence to make the big calls.

If your island of comfort is the place where you don't have to take a view on things, you will be missing the bigger opportunity. Without an opinion, you will be stuck on the island. You won't be noticed, because you haven't dared to say what you think about the wider world. You've got to be bold enough to push the boat away from the island into the uncertain currents.

Belief and opinion also give you motivational ENERGY – the next important principle we'll look at.

Summary

- **Have a view:** As a leader, decisiveness is a premium quality. You demonstrate it by forming opinions and sticking to them. The opinion is what helps you to cut through. It is what human audiences are looking for.

- **Don't list things:** Sadly, most business 'communication' is a list of things, but humans can't absorb lists very easily. Don't just list. Draw the strands together. Tell your audience what it means for them. Opinion is the currency of leadership communications.

- **Your view *is* the company view:** By all means have your own views, but don't imagine that these can be distinguished from the views of your business. The audience will struggle to separate the two.

4. ENERGY

This chapter explains the vital importance of ENERGY in communication, how we should seek out 'influencers' with good energy and why we should resist the temptation to 'go negative', even if it's an easier way to create a headline.

Energise

Without energy and enthusiasm for your subject, it's very hard to be a good communicator. Even if you do everything else in this book, your communications will be limp if there's no energy in the delivery.

PR for Humans requires energy.

Energy can also save you if your material is a bit of a mess or your story is a little tangled. Once you stand up and energise, a heck of a lot of flaws can be overlooked.

When I was at the BBC, I would often watch and listen back to my appearances on TV and radio. Sometimes I felt I'd done a flawless live interview with the presenter in the studio, but looking back at it I realised that the energy levels were a few notches below where they could have been. I was putting so much thought into the accuracy of the words that I failed to flick the big switch marked 'ENERGISE'.

You might imagine that the spotlight of a television studio or the sensitivity of a microphone requires a calm and subtle approach. You might think that every little nuance, tone and facial expression will be picked up. The key, you might imagine, is to be a slightly more focused and controlled version of yourself.

Well, perhaps this works for some individuals with extraordinary stillness and natural gravitas, but when I do media training, the most common feedback note I give is: be more energetic. That doesn't mean leaping around and doing lots of physical expression. It means concentrated, energetic thought and delivery, so that the audience will be able to feel the excitement you feel.

When was the last time you watched a business interview or video and thought, *whoa, that CEO/senior partner/analyst/economist has way too much energy! I wish they'd take it down a bit*? Almost never. It's far more common to think, *come on, give it a bit of life!*

This point was brought home to me – yet again – when I was coaching a partner at a business services firm ahead of an important keynote speech. I was, to be honest, worried about the material. The story he was trying to tell didn't seem clear enough. He was making too many points and using way too many slides for my liking. The call to action wasn't obvious. There weren't any good jokes or lighter moments. In short, this was a typically poor business speech waiting to be delivered. But despite all this, he bounded onto the stage and delivered his talk with sack-loads of energy. He looked happy and excited. He created electricity in that hall. The speech was decent – against the odds. He violated many of the principles of *PR for Humans*, but he (just) got away with it because of energy.

In the often exhausting and relentless world of business, those with energy are the leaders and the changemakers. Those who think carefully and reflect and methodically construct can be left behind. We naturally seek out those with the energy to convince others and solve problems. As the saying goes: 'If you want to get something done, ask a busy person'.

Energy doesn't mean we charge into the room or onto the stage and hurl our thoughts and opinions at others. It's more a state of mind. We can, I believe, *listen* with real energy, for instance, as I will discuss in later chapters.

Some lucky individuals have their natural energy levels set high. They seem to be able to power from one energised meeting to the next. For the rest of us, we need to think about how we store up our energy and release it at key moments – in the big speeches, the crunch meetings, the campaign launches and the critical presentations.

At these times, you need to increase the voltage.

Seek Influence

As well as tapping into our own reserves of energy, we need to seek out and surround ourselves with people who themselves possess good energy. You know the ones I mean. Think of your own life and your business contacts. Which people light up the room and brighten your day? Those with good energy aren't just a welcome tonic, they are also a critical part of your communications success. The audience is judging you by the company you keep. Those with good energy tend to be the influencers, so find them. And if you can, become one of them.

A few months into my PR career, the team in the agency were in a brainstorming session and the conversation got onto the subject of so-called 'influencers'. Normally in marketing and communications this refers to celebrities or trusted individuals who, through their endorsements or participation in a campaign, are able to generate some buzz and attention. If you want to be noticed, then enlisting the help of the already famous or respected is a time-honoured recipe for attention, even if some of the resulting coverage can feel a little shallow or off target.

We were grappling with the question: who in the world would you trust the most if he or she endorsed a campaign? It took one colleague only a few seconds to come up with an answer that was very hard to challenge.

"David Attenborough."

Yes, Attenborough is probably the ultimate media influencer. From childhood, his hypnotic voice has overlaid pictures of the most beautiful creatures and scenes on Earth. He is always on the side of the planet, never seeming to be in it for self-enrichment or to push a political message. Attenborough: the ambassador for our world, representing nature. Is there anyone with more natural good energy?

Attenborough has built his reputation by being a skilful broadcaster and truly loving his subject. But also, he's done it through association. In effect, he borrowed his energy and reputation from all the plants and animals of our planet. It's very hard to criticise him without being somehow against our own Earth.

Of course, Attenborough would not be available for the mortgage awareness campaign we were planning (or whatever it was – I must confess I have forgotten). But, extraordinarily, Attenborough *was* about to sign up for another campaign that I was fortunate enough to lead in 2015, just a few weeks later.

Circumstances had brought me together with Lord (Richard) Layard and Lord (Gus) O'Donnell – two extremely eminent members of 'the great and the good' – who, together with Sir David King, had come up with something they were calling the Global Apollo Programme. The idea was to encourage the governments of the world to plough billions of dollars into renewable energy research. They argued that a global government-sponsored technology push could dramatically lower the cost of generating, storing and transmitting clean energy.

Lord Layard had come to know David Attenborough and, using his unique powers, had somehow persuaded the world's greatest naturalist to lend his support. Attenborough liked the simplicity of the idea, and the fact that it was an environmental movement that wasn't asking us to *stop* doing things. It wasn't a call to stop driving, shopping, consuming food or taking holidays. Instead, Global Apollo was entirely focused on technology. If the generation, storage and transmission costs of renewable energy fell below the costs of fossil fuels, then oil and gas would simply stay in the ground. Using the name 'Apollo' was, of course, a reference to the Moon landings programme. The common theme was that, if you can bring some of the best scientific minds together and give them an impossible-sounding 10-year goal, amazing things can happen.

After one meeting with Gus O'Donnell, David King and some others, I was sitting with Richard Layard and talking about how we were going to take things forward ahead of the critical climate summit in Paris in December of 2015.

"I'll call David Attenborough," said Layard. *Ring ring.* Someone on the other end answered. "Hello, David. Yes, all well. I'm now passing you over to Mike Sergeant, who is running the campaign."

Still not quite believing that you can simply call David Attenborough at home and he'll pick up the phone straight away, I had to think fast. What was I going to say to him? What were we in fact asking the great man – then approaching his 90th birthday – to do? None of this had even been discussed properly. But I knew from my TV news days that the thing you need to do in these situations is confirm the person, the time and the location. Everything else can be figured out later.

"We'd like to come to your house next week to record a video for Global Apollo," I said.

"Fine," chirped Attenborough. "How about next Wednesday at 10?"

"Great. We'll be there!"

At that time we didn't have a script, a camera crew or any idea what we were going to do with the video or how it might be distributed. But we had the most important things. We had the story clear in our minds, as we had spent a week working out how to tell it. And we had our dream figurehead, our public face, the guy with the good energy.

Attenborough had indicated that he was comfortable with autocue, as you might expect from someone who has probably narrated more hours of television to more people than anyone else on Earth. So I set to work on the text. The words came easily. I had been listening to this man's phrases and delivery all my life. In under an hour, I had a script for David Attenborough!

When we arrived at his house, he took a few minutes to read over the script, and suggested changing a single (rather unimportant) word. He was completely charming – wonderfully similar to his TV persona – in a lovely house suitably bedecked with beautiful artefacts from his travels all over the world.

Richard and I then persuaded Attenborough to accompany us to the 2015 Paris summit in person for a final media blitz. Sir David told me that he had gone almost nine decades without attending an international summit. He was curious to see what all the fuss was about. He was energetic. He was indefatigable. In one 10-hour media blitz, he projected his wonderful personality and warmth across the world's assembled media. CNN, BBC, Bloomberg, CNBC, Sky News, Al Jazeera – we did the lot. He never tired, never lost his temper, never said, "Enough".

What stays with me is Attenborough's extraordinary energy and appetite for work. Even at the age of nearly 90, he was always up for doing another take, recording another interview, giving another quote. If you want to be a leader in any field, I guess the lesson is: it never comes easily or without effort. Everyone has to work. Even David Attenborough. You can never rest on past fame or previous achievements. The only thing that matters is your application today.

If you bring the right energy, find the right people, then you can influence. Especially if you stay positive.

Fear the Dark Side

In *Star Wars*, Yoda warns that fear leads to anger, anger leads to hate, and hate leads to suffering.

In PR – just like in *Star Wars* – there's the light side and the dark side. The tools can be used for good, moral purposes. Or they can be used by the forces of darkness. Great communicators don't have to be good people (but it's nice if they are). The techniques of rhetoric, audience manipulation and propaganda have been used by some of the biggest villains in history, and the easiest way to incite a strong response is to slide down the Yoda scale towards greater negativity and hatred.

That's the path of bad energy.

Terrible news always cuts through. Stories of extreme danger, pain and suffering grip audiences. In newsrooms, the old saying goes: 'If it bleeds, it leads'.

Humans are addicted to bad news. Death, destruction, disaster, scandal, resignation, chaos, collapse. These stories captivate us. Things often go wrong quickly, spectacularly and sometimes catastrophically. Progress, on the other hand, requires constant application and slow appreciation. It's often boring. People being nice to each other is boring. Conflict is more interesting. A career or a reputation takes years to build but moments to destroy.

Sometimes, audiences *need* to see and hear negative things. This is the only way to mobilise the 'goodies' and improve a bad situation. But there are always risks in the swirling negativity.

In parts of the social media universe, there is now a perpetual cycle of bile, outrage and hatred, punctured only occasionally by euphoria. Rivers of vitriol and drops of ecstasy. The world seems a more divided and cynical place than ever. People are bonding through anger and entrenching themselves in clefts of like-minded opinion. In this context, the dark side is absolutely something to be feared.

Sometimes clients ask me whether they should go positive or go negative. Tell a story of hope or a story of fear. This is a legitimate question in certain circumstances. The choice is sometimes whether to choose a 'burning platform' or a 'promised land' story. Here are a couple of (moderate) examples:

- If companies don't digitise fully, they won't exist in five years' time (burning platform)
- If companies digitise fully, they can unlock extraordinary new opportunities (promised land)

The burning platform stories are the easiest ones to tell. They are the ones that journalists will be most interested in. On the Yoda scale, they usually edge into the first section marked FEAR – if we don't do something, we're heading for disaster. My advice: resist the temptation of the negative angle.

In most situations, the consequences of negativity may be limited. But I think there's a wider moral dimension to this choice.

Slipping further towards the dark side can happen more easily than you might think, particularly in a world of inequality and injustice. Once we have generated some fear, the next step to ANGER is sometimes easy enough. If the threats to the business landscape are severe enough, people will move to the next level: HATE. Then it's time to put on the Darth Vader masks.

If you think I'm being excessive, remember some of the biggest business stories of recent years. It often begins with fear or mistrust of rapid change or excessive corporate power. Then comes the anger at the 'fat cats', media barons or tech billionaires. Whipped up by social media, outright hatred quickly follows in some quarters. Tides of opinion can quickly turn and strengthen.

Campaigners for social change often *need* to operate in the fear/anger part of the Yoda scale. You can't change the world simply by saying everything is lovely, people are gorgeous and the whole place smells of roses. You've got to fear something and be angry about something if you want to change something. The greatest struggles in history – racial equality, gender equality and LGBT rights – have come about because of a whole lot of anger. But even in the face of great injustice, anger doesn't have to become hatred. From Gandhi to Nelson Mandela, our most admired leaders have been the ones who've refused to hate, and managed – somehow – to forgive.

Political leaders will usually begin an election campaign by promising to stay positive. Then, as the weeks go by, the attack dogs are unleashed more frequently. By the time we get to polling day, hostility and negativity pervade.

Unfortunately, sometimes the negative energy wins. Fear beats hope. But given the moral aspect of *PR for Humans*, hand on heart, my advice must be: don't do it, however tempting it may be.

Business leaders can't usually venture even into the fear part of the scale, let alone all the way to anger or hate. They must stay way over on the light side, as eternal optimists and believers in progress. When I'm asked whether companies should put out a positive-sounding or a negative-sounding headline, my recommendation is always: stay positive. An 'attack' or a 'fight' or a 'row' is easier to sell as a news story, but this misses the point. I don't think business leaders – those with the massive responsibility of securing economic growth and providing jobs – can afford to play with red lightsabers. They've got to resist the temptations of the dark side at every turn. They must instead seek out good energy, within themselves and within others.

They must also always be looking upwards and outwards, seeing the wider CONTEXT, which is where the next chapter takes us.

Summary

- **Energise:** Energy counts for a heck of a lot in *PR for Humans*. Even a tangled story and the lack of a clear mission can sometimes be saved by an energetic performance. Humans move towards people with energy.

- **Seek influencers:** Your reputation will depend on the energy of those who surround you and associate with your activities. Seek out those with as much good energy as you can find. Borrow influence from them.

- **Stay positive:** In every news story, in every speech, you will face the question of whether to go positive or go negative. Going negative is the easiest route to coverage and impact. Humans have a fascination with the negative, but we want the positive. Staying relentlessly positive will ultimately be more valuable for you and your business.

5. CONTEXT

Here we explore the need to understand and talk about the CONTEXT in communication. You can't just speak about yourself and your organisation. You must look out at the horizon. Contemplate other businesses, the broader market and the wider world. Find allies who share your views.

Get off Your Island

As the poet John Donne wrote: 'No man is an island'.[4]

With *PR for Humans* storytelling, you need to look outwards as well as inwards.

You must understand the context. However interesting the central character (you) and the main organisation (your business), without the broader context the story may have limited appeal.

By context I mean the themes and currents out there in the world: the market, changing technology, political developments, consumer tastes, cultural changes and so on.

To be interesting, you need to be relevant. Capture the zeitgeist. Surf the waves. Break down barriers. Build bridges. Explore new territory. Have a sense of which way the wind is blowing.

The best communicators have the broadest horizons. They can voyage almost anywhere with a built-in GPS and a mind map of contextual themes. The worst communicators are limited to short walks, using the map of their own company's balance sheet.

Really successful start-up businesses are founded by setting out the context first, or the broader problem that their organisation is built to solve.

If you look at the best presentations by companies pitching for money, they are context heavy; the talk often begins with the context. A celebrated example is the presentation deck Airbnb used when pitching for its first $600,000 in 2009.[5] The company, as we all know, has gone on to become

---

[4] John Donne, *Devotions on Emergent Occasions*, Meditation XVII.
[5] Freely available online, for example at: www.slideshare.net/ryangum/airbnb-pitch-deck-from-2008

a multi-billion-dollar global powerhouse. But the original presentation was incredibly simple:

- It started with the **problem**: hotels are expensive and leave you disconnected from cities. No easy way exists to book rooms directly with locals.
- It went on to outline the **market** size and potential. This is the big contextual dimension for any business. Here the numbers were punchy (but nothing compared with the reality that transpired).
- Only then came the **solution** and the description of the **platform**.

Airbnb succeeded because it started with an understanding of the contextual problem that a smart app might be able to solve. The rest is history.

The reason the business sections of most newspapers are sometimes rather dull is that each article typically focuses on one person or business. Unless you happen to be a shareholder, employee or customer of that firm, the news is boring. The best business journalists are the ones who can join the dots and tell us how this announcement fits into a bigger pattern. What does it tell us about the changing world out there?

If your annual results document is simply a list of everything you've done as an organisation over the past 12 months, that will be fine for the analysts who are paid to work out whether your company is valuable or in decline. For more neutral observers, however, it will all be forgotten or, more likely, ignored.

Because we are all immersed in our immediate world day in, day out, we can become very insular. This is one of the biggest problems I encounter in my media training and leadership coaching work. The participants spend a long time talking about themselves, their businesses and their immediate preoccupations. The big challenge is to get them off their islands, scanning the broader horizon and making more ambitious mental journeys.

Connect to the world outside by thinking of the context.

Draw Concentric Circles

One of the techniques I use to bring out the context is to draw the business story as a set of concentric circles.

- **The innermost circle:** This is your business. The things you do every day. The people you hire. The products you launch. The deals you close. The earnings you generate for your shareholders.

- **The second circle:** This is where your immediate competitors sit. Are you going head to head with them in some situations? Are you vying for the attention of the same customers? What makes you different?
- **The third circle:** This is your market. It's the sector that you operate in. Here your story needs to focus on trends and predictions for this market. How is it changing? What will successful businesses need to do in this sector to survive and thrive? You must be *the authority* on your sector.
- **The outermost circle:** This is the world. The biggest circle may include politics, technology, cultural change, demographics, urbanisation, inequality. These are the themes and issues that set the broadest (possibly global) context for your business.

Journalists – and those who are not directly connected to your company as employees, customers or shareholders – will be most interested in the outer rings. They will seek out business people who can give them an interesting perspective on the broadest range of issues. Failing that, they will look to those who can provide the most interesting take (including trends and future predictions) on the market that you are part of. They will always want to use you as the example of the bigger idea.

You are the case study. You are there to illustrate something bigger. By yourself you are not very interesting (sorry) unless you represent a massive, market-dominating company. When you stand up to speak at a conference, if you stay in the first and second circles, your talk will have limited appeal. But if you can reach to the outer circles, you will be cutting through to a much larger and more powerful audience.

Nigel Wilson, CEO of Legal & General, is an example of a CEO who has stepped well outside of his comfort zone and been rewarded for it. He could have simply stuck to the narrow world of the insurance industry, but – in his blog, speeches and media interviews – he gives views on subjects as diverse as social housing, renewable energy, the future of capitalism and devolution. In all of his interventions, there's a strong sense of *why*. All of these issues are (loosely) relevant to L&G as an investor in all parts of the UK economy. What sets Wilson apart is his ability to see the broad context.

Wilson was handed the accolade of top FTSE 100 communicator in 2014 because he stepped outside his industry boundaries to challenge politicians and other business leaders. The two previous winners were Sainsbury's boss Justin King in 2013 and Unilever chief Paul Polman in 2012, both of whom inhabited the outer rings. They always saw the context and carried wider responsibilities on broader shoulders.

When telling your story, try starting with the outer ring. For example:

- "Technology is driving incredible change. Here's how it affects our market. Here's how it affects us."
- "Demographic change is the most powerful force in the world economy. Here's what it means for our sector. Here's what it means for our business."
- "Inequality is the greatest single threat to the market economy. In our sector, those that do X will thrive, so for us it means..."

Starting with the outermost ring gives you the thing that all leaders should prize: relevance in the world.

Put the Customer in the Middle

The customer exists in the outer ring. They are in the real world, not the industry or market or organisation you inhabit. But successful business leaders *think* of their customers as being right inside the tightest circle.

In leadership communications, your customers are always in the audience. Whether you are speaking to employees, regulators, suppliers or politicians, frame things through the eyes of your customers (or clients) and you can't go too far wrong.

'The customer is always right' is the timeless business mantra. For decades, those on the shop floor might have paid lip service to this idea, while the board members and shareholders would be busy furthering a much grander agenda involving lofty concepts like strategy, expansion and market share. The customer was simply someone to be analysed, engaged and sometimes squeezed, while the real work of business continued: generating handsome returns for corporate leaders and investors.

Happily, this pyramid of faceless, powerless customers on the bottom and corporate titans on their lofty thrones far above has been turned on its head. The internet revolution, accompanied by the rise of social media, has put unprecedented power in the hands of the customer. Customers now have the ability – through posting, videoing and commenting – to shift the terms of brand engagement.

The internet gives customers the information and context they need to make choices in much more sophisticated ways. They're no longer choosing between, say, two high street shops, but between hundreds or even thousands of online sellers, each of which needs to compete for their attention and avoid their one-star reviews.

We have entered a customer-centric age, an age of changing consumer expectations accompanied by a spirit of activism and supported by the new digital tools. Customers are creating data and using it – every minute of every day. For businesses, everything must now be oriented around the customers' needs. People are enjoying a golden age of gadgetry, instant communication and apparently boundless information.

But we are also in danger of being swamped. No customer can consume and interpret the millions of pieces of content that are sprayed out every day. For businesses to survive and thrive in this rapidly changing, customer-centric world, they need to think differently. The customer experience and journey are paramount. Those ultimately buying the products want a smooth and personal experience. Businesses need to deliver this personalisation at a massive scale, across all channels and geographies.

This is the context now for consumer-facing businesses, and to an extent all businesses. They need to think of their story by thinking about who their customers really are. Not as numbers on an annual report, but as real human beings, with hopes, interests, fears and concerns.

The story context for business must now be framed around the customer. If it isn't, and we talk in abstract terms about markets and growth and revenues, without the human bit, then those customers will soon be gone. The customer age is a promiscuous time.

Find Allies

To keep people engaged – to reach for the context in the outer circles of your communication – you will often need allies. This chapter started with a quote from John Donne, 'No man is an island'. You can't just stand on the tiny islet of your company. You need partnerships. Often, as we said in earlier chapters, you will look to people with demonstrable good energy to borrow influence from. Sometimes the allies are less obvious.

In the spring of 2007, during my time reporting in the Middle East for the BBC, I went from Jerusalem to Bethlehem to attend a very unusual rally. Normally we would cover demos held by others, but this time it was our campaign. We had a cause: Free Alan.

BBC Gaza correspondent Alan Johnston had been kidnapped by the Palestinian Army of Islam on the 12th of March. He was eventually released, unharmed, after four months in captivity. The Bethlehem demo took place about halfway through his kidnapping ordeal, and at the time we had no idea who exactly was holding him, or whether he was even alive.

I had met Alan Johnston once, a couple of months earlier, and had liked him immediately. I'd also listened to and admired his reports from Gaza for many months previously, as I prepared for my own assignments in the Middle East, so I felt I knew him much better than I did. For the whole of the BBC bureau in Jerusalem, it was a curious and emotional time. Their colleague was missing. They had to report on the facts of the story calmly and professionally *and* think of anything they could do to help to get Alan back.

So one day we got into our SUVs, loaded with cameras and radio kit, and drove to Bethlehem, where Palestinian journalists had gathered in Manger Square outside the Church of the Nativity. Alan Johnston was a popular figure among fellow reporters and bloggers in Gaza and the West Bank. The BBC was also, I felt, held in generally high regard. Yes, we were often criticised by either the Israeli or Palestinian leadership, but on the whole relations were positive. There was a lot of goodwill in Bethlehem that spring morning. I was about to find out just how much support we had, and from a very unlikely source.

As we unfurled our banners and started our 'Free Alan' chants, we took turns both being in the demo *and* reporting on it – recording interviews, pieces to camera and radio clips. Then, out of the corner of my eye, I spotted a group of heavily armed, bearded fighters marching towards the demonstration. *Uh oh, here comes trouble*, I thought. The BBC was nervous about further kidnappings of its staff, and these guys looked mean.

"Who are they?" I asked a Palestinian journalist standing nearby.

"Islamic Jihad," he answered.

The armed wing of Palestinian Islamic Jihad, called the Al-Kuds Brigades, was active in the West Bank and Gaza Strip. They are considered terrorists by many people, committed as the group is to the destruction of Israel.

The Al-Kuds fighters advanced towards our gathering, stopped, picked up posters... and joined the rally! Their chants were, I assume, some version of the 'Free Alan' slogans we were shouting. Their gruff voices filled the air as they held aloft banners, their automatic weapons slung over their shoulders.

It turns out the Islamic Jihad guys rather liked Alan Johnston. They considered his reports to be fair and balanced, including as they always did both sides of the story. Those heavily armed, bearded and scary-looking fighters thought Johnston's kidnapping a serious injustice. They wanted him freed.

And that was how, on that one day only, we found ourselves campaigning with the most unlikely of allies. At that precise moment, the BBC and Islamic Jihad shared a common objective, even if our world views were (under normal circumstances) wildly different. Eventually Alan was released because he had powerful supporters across the global media *and* among the powerful families who rule the streets in Gaza and the West Bank. The different layers and combinations of support were crucial.

The lesson I took from that day was that you need allies. Ninety-nine per cent of the time they will not be heavily armed militants, I would hope! But to succeed in communications, you need to know who can add weight to your cause and allow you to connect with audiences you'd never be able to reach on your own.

For campaigns to work, for businesses to break through in the way they communicate, alliances and partnerships are almost always needed. It's very hard for any individual, for any single business, to create and build a movement. Real success always comes from combinations. A single business shouting about itself will never be that interesting. But find allies to share your cause and the power multiplies.

One manifestation of this is the open letter, which can be sent to a newspaper, magazine or website and signed by multiple CEOs, academics, environmentalists or celebrities. Get enough credible people together who carry influence and can pull strings, and suddenly you are away. People will listen. Journalists will report your story.

Who are the most credible people to join forces with? Those with a keen understanding of where they've come from and where they're going. TIME is the principle we explore in the next chapter.

Summary

- **Reach out:** The best communicators have the broadest horizons. They're the ones who look outwards. They don't just talk about themselves or their company but connect to the wider context – in the market and the world. Humans respond to those who see the context.

- **Focus on the customer:** The customer is always at the heart of good business. They are out in the big world you are trying to reach. But emotionally they need to be at the very heart of it all. Frame your external communication in the context of their human wants and needs.

- **Find allies:** Connecting with the big themes and issues in the world can be difficult and daunting for one individual or one company. The right allies can help to multiply the power of your communication and reach much wider audiences.

6. TIME

In this chapter, the importance of TIME is emphasised. The reader will see how the best communicators are able to frame the past, the present and the future as the main elements of their own business stories.

Root Yourself

Practitioners of *PR for Humans* need to have a keen sense of time. The past, the present, the future. Where they were, where they are, where they are going.

'To begin at the beginning', wrote Dylan Thomas, in his famous opening to *Under Milk Wood*. I was lucky enough to play the part of First Voice, who delivers this line, in a student theatre production of the play in 1995. The words stay with me, as do many of Thomas's lyrical phrases in that wonderful work.

When telling your story, it's often important to talk about the past. The audience wants to know where you've come from. Your backstory gives you credibility and power. But your viewers and listeners won't know it if you don't tell them.

Begin at the beginning.

But when is the beginning? How far back should you go?

For the individual, you can go as far back as you like, if the experience you recount is relevant to the arc of the story. Sure, talk about something that happened to you at school, but make sure the listener understands why that is relevant for your business today. Mention your first job, if that experience taught you something about who you are now.

Reaching into the past must tell the audience something about your character in the present. How you got to be the person you are today.

Stories about your life may be:

- Character forming – somehow the experience changed you
- Turning points – moments of enlightenment that set you on a better path (these can be times of success or failure)

The best superhero films are the origin stories – the ones where the central character obtains or discovers their powers. We want to see where they came from and how they got to be the hero they are now. The sequels are always a disappointment once the individual is fully formed.

Show your origins. The audience wants to know a bit about your family background, so reveal your roots. Not all the time, but for the biggest moments when you need to make the deepest impressions.

Bill Clinton did this brilliantly in his acceptance speech at the 1992 Democratic Convention. He told the audience that his speech would be about giving hope to those who'd been left behind. First, Clinton told the audience how he'd never met his father, who was killed in a car crash. Then came this:

> When I think about opportunity for all Americans, I think of my grandfather. He ran a country store in our little town of Hope.

The speech built the theme around the central character of his grandfather, and ended with this famous line, that helped send Clinton to the White House:

> I end tonight where it all began for me: I still believe in a place called Hope.

To some people reading that now, the schmaltz might seem unbearable. In the hall at the convention centre in 1992, however, even the most cynical, hard-bitten journalists would have felt a powerful surge of warmth for the man on the stage.

The best storytellers always find ways of showing the audience where they've come from.

The great thing about an 'origin story' or 'turning-point story' is that it is unquestionably *yours*. You aren't borrowing, faking or imitating. In the search for authenticity, this is priceless.

We judge our leaders not only on their capabilities in the job, but also by the voyage they've been on. Was the passage easy or difficult? Did they come from affluence or poverty? Have they ever been tested in moments of danger or stress or jeopardy? Do they have the first-hand experience to tackle the job at hand?

For many in business, the deep 'life lessons' can seem rather soft and sentimental. Surely being a serious business leader is about maintaining professional rigour and discipline? You certainly don't want to take the misty-eyed nostalgia too far. But the trick is to combine your memories of the past with practical action in the present.

I would advise every business person to have one story about their family origins and maybe five or six stories about key moments in their past that gave them the experience to lead. Every situation will be different, but if you can find something in your career backstory that is particularly relevant to the audience you are standing in front of, that will hugely elevate the quality of your appearance.

Reach Back for Your Company Story

Speakers need a personal life story, but they also need to be able to tell the story of their company. These are two different things.

Corporate stories also need to be rooted in the past. The founding mission should, to some extent, still be the mission today. Again we need to ask the question: how far back in history should we go?

I've worked with a family-owned property business that has been going, in one form or another, for two centuries. I've also worked with a Japanese bank that traces its activities back over 300 years. While both stories give a wonderfully reassuring sense of timeless stability (withstanding wars, elections, natural disasters and profound technological change), they also limit the ability of these businesses to be seen as industry leaders. The question to ask is: does it matter? Sometimes it genuinely doesn't. But often it is a problem.

The one rule that I learnt as a reporter, and which is also relevant for corporate storytelling, is this: you can only go back in time once. So in a television report, for example, you can start with fresh, on-the-day pictures and then dive back into the 'file' or 'library' shots from last year or 20 years ago. Then you can come back to the present day. But you can't, and you mustn't, keep jumping backward and forward in time. Only the most skilful novelists can get away with doing this. In business, we can't. It's too confusing.

In corporate terms a 'going back once' story might be something like:

> We're a global bank, currently active in X markets with particular strengths in Y and Z. Of course, we have a very long and proud history, stretching back X hundred years. That helps us keep a long-term perspective and give our clients the sense that we're not just here to make a fast buck. In the current climate, with banks and financial institutions facing serious questions of trust, that commitment to the long term is unusual and, in my view, essential.

Present–past–present is usually a decent rule of thumb for the telling of a company story.

If the business is a relatively recent creation (say within the last 10 years) then we also have the opportunity to tell the 'start-up story', which journalists, investors and customers love.

The 'start-up story' has many forms. It might be a chance encounter, a moment of epiphany, a technological breakthrough or simply a fabulous moment of creativity (with, say, the idea for a clever name or brand identity).

One of the best is the story of how FedEx came into being.[6]

The founder, Fred Smith, was an undergraduate at Yale. He wrote an economics paper in 1965 exploring transportation processes in the USA. He argued that a dedicated company could transport small, essential items by plane more efficiently than the existing network of truckers and passenger planes. The paper was graded a C. But Smith didn't give up and he launched Federal Express in 1971.

Within three years, however, the company was on the verge of bankruptcy and losing $1 million a month. Then Fred Smith broke all the rules. He reportedly went to Las Vegas with the company's last $5,000 and played blackjack with it. Smith came back with $32,000 – enough to cover the company's fuel costs for a few more days until institutional funding could be secured. Today FedEx has global revenues of $60 *billion*.

The story is amazing. And it's one of those 'got away with it once but never ever try this again' tales. Most start-up stories are a little less colourful. Another one that stands out and is remembered, however, is the Innocent Smoothies foundation story.[7]

The founders started Innocent after selling smoothies at a music festival. They put up a big sign and when people tried their smoothies they were asked to vote whether the team should give up their jobs to make them. The empties went into a 'yes' bin or a 'no' bin:

> At the end of the weekend, the 'Yes' bin was full, so we resigned from our jobs the next day and got cracking.

Every new business starts with an idea, the trigger that sends the founders on their way. Some of these events may have dragged on for weeks, months or years until the entrepreneurs finally plucked up the courage to give it a go, or waited to have all the bits in place that they needed. However, the story is

---

6 As reported and repeated by multiple sources, including *Forbes* and *Business Insider*.
7 Innocent's start-up story, as told on the company website: www.innocentdrinks.co.uk/us/our-story

usually better if presented as one 'ah ha!' lightbulb moment. Audiences love big, decisive actions, particularly if there is a large element of risk involved.

Even if your business seems purely functional, designed simply to provide a standard service for clients or sell products in an obvious market, there is a story lurking somewhere. As well as the moment of inception, there will be other important milestones along the way. When putting together your corporate story, look back over the past 10 years and ask: when were the breakthroughs? What were the transformative moments? How did you respond when the business was tested in some way? When did you decide to launch a new branch of activity? These questions will provide a timeline to inform your story.

But remember that *the timeline isn't the story*. Too many company websites have a list of dull corporate events and acquisitions or demergers. These are tedious and probably never read. Better to use one or two moments that make the biggest statement about the identity, values or ambition of the business.

Ideally – and this isn't always possible – the corporate story will overlap with the personal story, each reinforcing the other. If you're newer to the firm then smoke and mirrors are sometimes needed to bring your key moments together with those of the business in ways that don't jar, particularly if you've been hired from a competitor.

However (and more on this later in Part 1, Chapter 7 on humility), your company story can't just be a playlist of your greatest hits.

If your corporate narrative is a sequence of 'we did this brilliantly, then we did that cleverly, then we won that thing, then we conquered that market', the audience will be already going to fetch their coats.

Good stories about the past contain struggle and failure. Tension must come before triumph – if indeed triumph comes at all.

Be Present

As well as thinking about the past, we need to focus on the present. The moment. Where the action is. Right now.

I think of the first time I met Tony Blair.

I had been waiting at a large East London primary school for an hour or two with the camera crew, getting the shots we needed for a television piece on the lunchtime news about the government's education announcements.

The Downing Street press officer supervised us as we found a decent spot to set up for the interview with the prime minister. After lots of scurrying backward and forward by various fixers and hangers-on, a Jaguar pulled up outside. The photographers jostled for position.

Time was tight. The press officer was, as usual, looking frazzled. He ordered us to stay put and said that he would escort the PM around the building. We were told we would only have five minutes for the interview.

Then Tony Blair walked calmly and purposefully into the room and up to the camera.

"OK, let's go," he said with his trademark grin.

This was late on in his premiership: after the invasion of Iraq, but before the aftermath of the conflict took a heavy toll on the man many had embraced with such excitement in 1997 when New Labour swept to power.

The impression he gave the day I interviewed him was of a man completely in control. Absolutely comfortable at the present moment in time. On top of his brief. Not seeming to carry any baggage. Completely focused. Completely present.

When we talk about 'presence' in a leadership context, it means that the person somehow changes the room when they enter it. This may be to do with fame. It may be to do with power. It is also to do with owning the present. Being, as they say, 'in the moment'. That's charisma.

Blair was all those things that day. His soundbites were smooth, though of course I can't remember them now. What I do remember, however, is the feeling he created. This is so often the case with our recollection of leaders: the impression they give out *is* the memory. Long after the analysis and context are forgotten, the emotional imprint remains.

Journalists are obsessed with the present. The question is always: what's the story *today*? The story from the morning radio bulletin will have changed by lunchtime. The version for the evening news will be completely different again. So much will have happened. Things will have moved on with dizzying speed.

Yesterday's stories are easily forgotten. History is fascinating but often remote. What may happen in the future is sometimes hard to grapple with now. But the present, today, the new stuff, the decisions that are being made, the announcements of the moment – that's news.

We spend so much of our lives thinking about the past and worrying about the future. Sometimes the hardest part is to live in the present and enjoy *this* moment in time. We can't change the past and we often struggle to predict the future. The present is the bit we can control – though, for some reason, we are often reluctant to seize the moment and enjoy it.

While journalists naturally connect with the on-the-day story, those in business sometimes struggle to see it. Maybe it's too obvious because it's right in front of them.

When I'm doing media training, the questions I ask are: what is the *new* thing here? What is your opinion about the new thing? The story you tell must contain the latest information. It must be different to the story you told last year. It must be the story for this present moment in time.

A list of performance numbers (profit, loss, revenue) is a historical record. A strategy is the plan for how you are going to fight the battles ahead. But the most compelling action is often in the present-day plotline rather than the flashback or the future dreamscape.

Leaders can't be comfortable if they are engrossed in historical anxieties or dreams of retirement or moving to another job. The impression you must give is that *this* job, at *this* time is the point of maximum focus.

We mustn't forget our roots. But there is no time like the present.

The present gives us our energy. If we transmit the sense – in every meeting we attend, speech we give or interview we take part in – that nothing matters more than this point in time, our story will be much more compelling because we will be people of action.

In business and in politics we respect those who can connect with the moment and not be somehow absent. This may be for moments of positive or negative news. Triumphs or disasters. If a crisis strikes, the most important thing we want from our leaders is to be there. On the scene. Taking decisions. Taking responsibility. Across the latest developments. Even if things have gone badly wrong, the sense of current action and response can be powerful.

Lead Your Company's Action

The story you tell about your company must be firmly set in the present tense. Yes, the historical context and sense of direction are essential, but those following the story need to be told what the latest chapter is. What has the business done in this quarter? What's the most recent update? How is the firm responding to current developments in the market? Who has recently joined? What do the current acquisitions tell us about where the business is today?

Those running communications for companies – whether in agencies or in-house – need to be in-the-moment people, immersed in the very latest developments in the business, the sector and the wider economy. However great the origin story or the strategic direction, the handling of daily events and management of the news flow are still big determinants of reputation.

When management changes, there is a window of opportunity to put even more focus on the present. A new CEO or chair must give the diagnosis of where the organisation is *right now*, for good or ill.

Sometimes the present can seem almost too obvious because it is right in front of us. The temptation is to spend too much time talking about what happened a year or several months ago, or to cut straight to the 'vision' without the here and now.

The present, though, always matters in communication. The on-the-day story is always critical when leaders stand in front of their audiences. References to events happening in the news today can make business speeches and interviews more interesting and relevant.

As well as showing their roots and giving us the action of the present moment, however, leaders must also have a sense of where they are going. They need to own the future. And that is where we are heading next.

Be the Future

I want to talk about the future. He was the future once.[8]

That was the devastating put-down from newly elected Conservative leader David Cameron to prime minister Tony Blair when the two first clashed in the House of Commons in 2005.

The message was powerful and clear to those of us watching in the BBC's Millbank newsroom: your time has gone, mine has arrived.

On that day, at that time, Cameron was taking ownership of the future – something the most impressive leaders do in their speeches, debates and interviews.

A few weeks earlier, I'd been in the hall at the Conservative Party Conference in Blackpool when the Conservative candidates had all had to make a single 20-minute speech. Until that time, David Davis had been the clear frontrunner, but he made a very poor speech. His jokes fell flat, his delivery was wooden and he seemed uncomfortable at the podium.

Then David Cameron took to the stage with a masterly demonstration of confidence. Cameron spoke fluently and without notes. Taking his cue from the New Labour playbook, Cameron's speech was all about how the party must change to secure future success.

[8] David Cameron vs Tony Blair, Prime Minister's Questions, 7 December 2005, House of Commons.

58

As each of Cameron's 20 minutes went by, I had a stronger and stronger feeling that I was watching the next prime minister in action. You could feel the buzz in the hall. Energy. Relief. Excitement. The live TV cameras panned to the audience. They were alive. Laughing. Cheering. One speech was changing politics and changing history in front of our eyes. David Cameron had arrived. The man who would, after three election defeats, lead the Tories back to power.

Just as Tony Blair had used his skills as a platform speaker to drag the Labour Party over hot coals along the path to power, Cameron used a single 20-minute talk to turn the accepted order on its head, to let the world know that he was the coming man.

Was it a great speech? Was Cameron a master orator? Possibly not. But he did the simple things very well. He was a candidate who seemed to know exactly where he was going and how he was going to get there. At times of uncertainty and drift, this is a powerful elixir.

Of course, all political careers end in disappointment, to a certain degree. Having lost a botched referendum on the EU, David Cameron resigned. In his last appearance as prime minister in the House of Commons in 2016, he delivered a neat and self-deprecating bookend to his time at the top of British politics:

> Nothing is impossible if you put your mind to it. As I said at the beginning: I was the future once.

When politicians are struggling, they lose the ability to own the future. Leaders who are clinging on must spend their whole time putting out the day-to-day fires and finding ways to keep their enemies and rivals at bay. If you are likely to be gone tomorrow, power quickly seeps away. But the certainty that you've seen the future, planned for it and will be the person to take us there – that can be irresistible.

Describe Your Company's Future

Every business plan will include a set of projections for how fast the company will grow, the size of the market, the future levels of profitability and the expected growth of the workforce. When companies are small they want to give a sense of solidity and certainty about the future.

However, the reality, as any investor knows, is that these are shaky estimates – a finger in the air. More often the venture capitalists or early-stage investors will buy an idea, and their investment will reflect their confidence in a team of people to deliver it. They know that the dotted line on the graph covering the months and years ahead means very little.

Larger businesses will have more certainty about their market and their record of growth. But future projections are almost always extrapolations of the past, unless the company has embarked on a radical change of direction or is under new leadership. And even then, the shape of the horizon is really anyone's guess.

Targets are sometimes hit, either through good fortune or because they were set with a distinct lack of ambition. Often they are missed, sometimes by the width of a bus. The ability of managers to control numerical outcomes is limited at the best of times. Circumstances quickly change, and too many imponderables mean that today's goals can so easily become hostages to fortune. Better not to be too specific about outcomes in the future, lest you disappoint those you most need to believe in the trajectory.

Sometimes politicians set targets – for reducing class sizes, reducing hospital waiting times or other arbitrary measures of success. Some are hit, some are missed. Tony Blair's New Labour was particularly fond of doing this, believing targets to be almost sacred expressions of accountability. The problem was that, to meet one measure of success, another would be pushed under the carpet and out of sight. In the end the main political parties in the UK decided that it was better not to set any firm numerical targets on most policy outcomes.

Economic forecasts, including (and especially) those by official bodies like the Treasury and the Bank of England, are equally unreliable. In recent years, they have been absurdly inaccurate. Just as the famous BBC weather forecaster Michael Fish failed to predict the 1987 hurricane which swept across England, so the Bank of England failed to forecast the biggest financial storms of recent times. The Bank's chief economist, Andy Haldane, admitted as much at an event in London in 2017.

On that occasion, the Bank *had* forecast a hurricane in the wake of the Brexit referendum. But instead of a violent storm, there was a pleasant, warm wind from the direction of the continent. When questioned on this, Mr Haldane conceded, "It's true... fair cop."[9]

Forecasting really is too difficult, so resist the temptation to do it. Those people we think of as having a 'vision' don't fall into the numbers trap. They stick to the broad brushstrokes. The issues. The big themes. The trends. The story.

---

[9] As reported by the BBC, among others: www.bbc.co.uk/news/uk-politics-38525924

The future is about emotion. Hope.

Having a lack of specific targets, happily, makes for better and more interesting communication. Consider these two statements:

- "We want to increase the size of our property fund returns by 1% in year one, 2.5% in year two and 3.5% for all subsequent years".
- "We are on the cusp of a significant property upswing. The nature of the market in country X is fundamentally changing. We predicted it and we are perfectly well positioned to reap the benefits".

The targets in the first statement are completely random and, to my mind, lacking in substance or credibility. The second statement might be vague, but it comes closer to the thing that most audiences are crying out for: opinion. We want *a view about the future*. Targets and forecasts always create huge question marks for me. They are an attempt to be certain about something it is impossible to be certain about.

But here you must balance between optimal *PR for Humans* and *PR for Spreadsheet Officers*. Unfortunately, investors often want the future details and projections laid out in a serious-looking business plan. Their desire for professional-looking forecasts may override the truth: it's *always* a leap of faith. Think of the real buccaneers of industry. Have they made endless careful forecasts? Or have they made big, sweeping, gut-clenching moves?

One of the best business stories is that of Jack Ma, who grew up without money in communist China. He failed his college entrance exams. He was rejected from dozens of jobs, including one at KFC. He started two businesses that failed, before going on to establish the giant internet and technology company Alibaba. When the vast business floated, Ma became the richest man in China. The secret of his success? An unwavering belief in the future. Ma says he believed that younger generations could succeed in new ways, in a changing world powered by technology.

In a speech in 2014, this is how Ma described it:

> I called myself a blind man riding on back of blind tigers. Those experts who were riding horses, they all fell. We survived because we worried about the future. We believed in the future. We changed ourselves.[10]

An unknown future can be scary, which is why most of us are happy to stay in the present and keep doing the things we've been doing. We're not

---

[10] Jack Ma speaking to the Asia Society in 2014: www.youtube.com/watch?v=KDHPaHpDOl8

prepared, like Jack Ma, to 'ride on blind tigers'. We're happy to stroll along behind as the tiger-riders roar ahead to death or glory.

But when a woman or man steps up into the top job, they have to ride the tiger. Ultimately, success follows those who don't let fear stop them – those who put on the blindfold, climb onto their wild beasts and move forward. They will inherit the future.

Past, Present, Future – Do It All

Good communication or rhetoric appeals to the head, the heart and the gut. We make analytical (head) judgements about the things people are doing. We make character (gut) judgements about where people have come from and what they've done. We make emotional (heart) judgements about whether they can lead us to the promised land.

A similar formulation was used by the Ancient Greek philosopher Aristotle when he spoke of logos, ethos and pathos over 2,300 years ago:[11]

- Ethos – authority and character
- Logos – facts and figures
- Pathos – emotions

What leaders have done in the *past* can give them their integrity. This supports their character.

What leaders do in the *present* displays their actions, how logically they are tackling the problems of the moment.

What leaders want to do in the *future* is their vision. This is the emotional bit, where they ask for trust about the unknowable.

Past. Present. Future.

Ethos. Logos. Pathos.

Beginning. Middle. End.

Those doing *PR for Humans* will think about all three.

Control Time

When I think back to the impressive leaders in politics and business that I have seen in person – such as Tony Blair, Bill Clinton and David Cameron – they all appeared to be in control of time. Like great footballers who seemed to have 'time on the ball', they were absolutely in the moment, but they also had a solid backstory and a clearly mapped path to the future. They weren't

---

[11] As outlined in Aristotle's *Rhetoric*.

being rushed forward or backward by external forces. If they wanted to pause, they paused. If they wanted to up the tempo, they did and they could. I think they got this time-controlling quality from immense self-belief. But also, I think, from feeling deep down that they had the answer. Theirs didn't have to be the cleverest solution or the most popular course of action. The key was that *they* believed in it. Their communication power came from a deep connection to their material.

Most leaders will have nothing like the human qualities of David Attenborough, Oprah Winfrey or Barack Obama. (Although one CEO did tell me that he wanted to be the "David Attenborough of economics". I nearly spat out my coffee. I may be good at my job, but I'm not that damn good, mate!) But even if such goals are ridiculously unrealistic, we can all learn lessons by thinking about who we admire, in business, politics or any other field. Who would we like to be a bit more like? Watching others with a critical and positive eye is one of the most important things we must do if we are to improve our own communication skills. We all know, instinctively, what works and what doesn't. Which types of people we like listening to and which ones bore us rigid. To improve our skills, we need to think about others and how they perform.

But – and here's the twist – we can't directly copy others or imitate them. Very few gifted individuals are talented enough 'actors' to fake their route to charisma. Most people simply have to be themselves. 'Authenticity' may have become a slightly overused buzzword, but it's important. You need to find a way of communicating that is sustainable across the minutes, hours, days and weeks of your professional life. Being able to turn it on for the occasional big moment may get you out of jail a few times, but it probably won't get you or your business to the very top.

To be authentic, we sometimes need to show a little vulnerability. Or at least HUMILITY, which is our next principle.

Summary

- **Show the past:** Your audience needs to see where you and your organisation have come from. In your speeches and interviews, you need to show your roots. That's what will give substance to your character and power to your human story.

- **Be in the present:** As a leader, you are also the man or woman of action. You've got to be present. Ask: what is new today? What is the story right now? What makes this week different to last week? The present tense is the place where real things happen. That's where the focus of *PR for Humans* needs to be.

- **Own the future:** The most charismatic leaders seem to know where they're going. They have the decisiveness to plot a future course and follow it. Owning the future is an emotional leap of faith. We can't predict it, and yet we follow those who seem to possess it.

7. HUMILITY

This chapter looks at why HUMILITY can give us power in communication. We'll understand the Storyteller's Paradox (it's about you, but it can't be all about you) and see that to be heard, sometimes we need to talk less.

Be Humble

In communications, it's good to know what you don't know.

Enjoy humility. It can give you power. It's an important principle of *PR for Humans*.

When the CEO steps onto the conference platform or into the broadcast studio, we don't need or want to hear from a perfect specimen. The best leaders are open about some of their failures and mistakes. It's OK not to know all the answers and not to succeed every time. It took Edison thousands of attempts to try to make a lightbulb. After each attempt he said he hadn't 'failed', he just hadn't – yet – found a way to make it work.

Own your flaws. Nobody is perfect. Pretending to be reduces your influence. This is particularly important in the age of pretend social media perfection. With all the beautifully pictured lives played out on Instagram and Facebook, how refreshing when some imperfections are put on display.

As humans, we respond well to those who can be humble, show a little bit of modesty and demonstrate to the world that they are still learning and striving. Being arrogant and a know-it-all will create a significant barrier between you and any audience you are trying to reach. If our leaders seem too manicured or self-assured, we will smell a rat. This is even more true in the era of social media, when there is such value in demonstrable authenticity.

Sitting in the audience, we are painfully aware of our *own* mistakes, failures and ignorance about many of the big issues of the day. Human intelligence is often narrow and fleeting. Unless we are nerdy polymaths, each of us has proper knowledge of a relatively small slice of the world's information. Even then, our knowledge must be continually refreshed or it slips away. We judge the person leading – the person on the stage – with reference to our own limitations. If they claim to have none, we suspect them immediately.

Being humble isn't about wearing cheap clothes, living in a small house and never flying business class. It's more to do with self-awareness – acknowledging mistakes and being honest with the audience about your capabilities. That must, however, be combined with an almost fanatical desire to learn and improve. We must be open about failure but never accept it. Where there are problems, they must be addressed. Where standards are sloppy, they must be improved.

This can only be done if we have a connection with our audience.

Think about the expression 'I'm going to level with you'. In other words, I'm going to tell you something which is true, honest and revealing. I like the visual quality of this line, because that is what good leadership communication entails: *getting onto the same level as the audience*. Not talking down to anyone. Not nervously looking up to anyone. But looking straight across.

One of the problems with the classic CEO video – filmed in the boardroom and then emailed out to all corners of the company – is that it usually feels like a stiff message from on high, which immediately creates a division between the leader and the employees. Far better to get around the company with as many face-to-face briefings and team meetings as you can. It's time consuming, yes, but worth it for the connections you will forge.

Ask yourself, am I communicating *across*? Does it seem like I am on the same level as the people I am trying to reach?

Simple things can make a difference.

If there is a queue in the staff canteen at lunchtime and you are the CEO, go and stand in the queue. If there is a staff shuttle bus, take it sometimes and don't always roar past in your BMW. If you are leading a meeting, hear the opinions and grievances of others first, before making your own pronouncements.

Level with your audience. Show humility. It will win you trust and respect.

Understand the Storyteller's Paradox

Mistakes, embarrassments and failures make for interesting tales. In novels and dramas, the hero rarely has a simple route to victory. There are usually significant setbacks and challenges on the path to eventual success, if it comes at all.

This is a nice example from Allan Leighton's book, *On Leadership*.

As a young manager at Mars, Leighton was giving a speech to an underperforming sales team. He delivered what he thought was a brilliant address about raising standards and pushing harder to meet targets. But then, pausing for effect, he managed to spill his tea all over his shirt and trousers. Cue a huge eruption of laughter and, crucially, a change in the atmosphere:

> The whole relationship and our way of working changed. What's more, so did the sales figures.[12]

The key to a good story is that the challenges somehow change the main character and reveal their humanity. Through their trials, the hero emerges as a slightly different, ideally better person. But never perfect.

Which brings us to what I call the Storyteller's Paradox:

- It's got to be about you. To be effective your story must be personal and connect with your life.
- It can't be all about you. If you stuff your story full of ego, you will fail. The audience will dislike and distrust you.

Solving the Storyteller's Paradox is, I think, at the heart of good communication. The key to unlocking it is humility. Nobody likes to be lectured at by an arrogant so-and-so. We like our leaders to show some human frailty. We also want them to show us how they've overcome challenges and, crucially, learnt from *other people* at every turn.

Humility, a constant desire to learn, empathy, inquisitiveness, a determination to improve – these are the qualities that effective business leaders have. The stories we tell about our lives must be designed to demonstrate these assets. And in this, so much is about the style and tone of our writing. We can take exactly the same anecdote and make it sound graceful and wise, or arrogant and shallow. The words we choose make all the difference.

I made the mistake of ignoring humility early on in my coaching career. One client gave me a wonderfully colourful series of anecdotes and key moments from a brilliant life. *I'm away here*, I thought. *This is a dream assignment – the stories tell themselves!* But when I condensed the anecdotes and played them back to him, he sounded like the most self-centred jerk you could imagine. However, with a few tweaks to the language, he came across as a calm and self-deprecating guru.

---

[12] Allan Leighton, *On Leadership* (Random House Business: 2008).

Now I always keep the Speaker's Paradox in mind and try to work out where the line is between the personal stuff which audiences love, and the hubristic gunk which people despise.

Solve Someone's Problem

However brilliant and engaging you are, cutting through in business is often about solving someone's perceived problem, rather than entertaining them. This is, I believe, one important difference between business storytelling and other forms of storytelling. Yes, we are looking for ways to connect, using some of the principles all good storytellers use. But getting noticed in the commercial world is about coming along at exactly the right time to *be the solution*, sometimes to a problem people didn't even know they had.

When we're building corporate stories, we should always think about our audiences and the problems they have now, or might have in the future.

I think a lot of businesses have this slightly wrong. They go on and on about their unique selling point (USP), as if the most important thing in business is to do something completely new or original and then 'sell' that as hard as possible to customers. After decades of people being 'marketed at' and 'sold to' ever more aggressively, I think it's getting harder and harder to cut through with a sales pitch. Yes, you can define yourself against the opposition, but it's much better to think of yourself as a great problem-solver than a great salesperson.

I know now, from my own experience in business, that you rarely get hired because you are brilliant, intelligent, entertaining or incisive. You get hired when you come along at exactly the right moment to solve somebody's problem. Or you get hired because you can explain a problem to somebody with perfect clarity, giving them confidence that you will be able to find a solution.

We purchase things because we think we have a problem. Some common problems are: boredom, hunger, thirst, feeling cold or feeling wet. Some more complex problems could be: how to secure investment returns, how to calculate tax liabilities or how to structure a business. When companies produce marketing materials or create public relations content, it's a good idea to take a step back and ask: what's the core problem that we are trying to solve for our customers? What are their biggest challenges and concerns? What really annoys and irritates them? Then think: how can our story be an antidote to their hassle?

Business people often love the (sometimes violent) language of commerce. They speak of wanting to 'disrupt markets', 'break the mould' and 'hurt the competition'. Business is a competitive fight, in their minds, where everyone is trying to be bigger, better, more disruptive and more ruthless than everyone else.

How much more, though, do we like the elegant problem-solvers? The businesses and business people who are on the side of the customers, rather than constantly trying to take chunks out of their competitors? Those who are trying to smooth the world for us, rather than smash bits of it up?

The future belongs to those who can see our problems clearly and design easy and affordable solutions to those problems. In our increasingly stretched and frenetic lives, theirs are the stories we will gladly receive.

Want Something

Don't confuse being humble and being a problem-solver with a lack of ambition. Showing your desires is a good thing, generally.

Leaders shouldn't just be ambitious in the abstract sense. They need to want something specific. Once they do – and are seen to – their character will make a lot more sense to the audience.

We understand up-and-coming politicians because we assume they want a seat in the Cabinet or want to become prime minister. We understand that senior directors in a professional services firm want to become partners in the business. We understand that the chief financial officer might one day want to become the CEO.

The clarity of the ambition defines the character. That doesn't mean they need to go around incessantly describing their goal – in fact, it's better not to. But it's hard to watch a game with any interest if the fans don't know what the player is trying to achieve.

When we read a book or watch a film, the central character typically wants something. In a rom-com, they want the girl (or boy). In fantasy quest stories, they want the mythical object. In horror stories, they want to kill the alien/zombie/monster. In stories about power, they want to become the president/crime boss. In cop shows, they want to catch the criminal.

The leading character always wants something, or there's no story.

Here's how Aaron Sorkin, writer of *The West Wing*, *Steve Jobs* and *The Social Network* put it:

> If the character doesn't want anything, they are probably cluttering up
> your script and you don't need the character.[13]

Without a clear desire, a character is passive. In novels, plays and movies we look for the protagonist. The word comes from the Greek *protos* (first in importance) and *agonistes* (person engaged in a struggle). If you are to be the lead character in your own show, the struggle must be apparent to your spectators. They must be able to see what you want.

This is different from caring about something or believing in something. This is the personal bit. The desire must be *for you*. Not for the company or your customers or the planet – *you*. And it can't be too woolly. We can't simply want 'success' or 'power' or 'money' or 'love'. We must define the ambition much more tightly if the struggle is to have any meaning.

All good drama is based on character. Without characters, there is no story. The plot is just what happens to the characters and how they are changed by the experiences. As the CEO or business leader, you have been handed the lead role, but the show can still be a flop if your desire isn't clear.

As the Greek philosopher Heraclitus said, 'Character is destiny'.[14] This implies that destiny, or fate, is not determined by outside forces. It comes from within. Your character. What you believe. What you want.

Many philosophers might disagree, arguing that the only things we can control are our thoughts and actions. We can't control outcomes, so it's useless to desire them. That may be correct. But in business, even if we can't control the future, we need to be seen to be trying to shape it. We need to show what we want.

We see this idea manifested in many different artistic guises.

The Russian actor and theatre director Konstantin Stanislavski, for instance, is credited with unlocking the *desire* that a convincing character must display, which he called the 'objective'. You can't act unless you know *why* the character is doing something. What do they want? What (or who) do they desire? How do they want to achieve what Stanislavski called the *zadacha* (which translates as 'goal' or 'task')?[15] The actor who doesn't know the answers to these questions complains to the director that they don't understand the character's 'motivation'.

---

[13] Aaron Sorkin, screenwriting masterclass: www.masterclass.com/classes/aaron-sorkin-teaches-screenwriting

[14] As attributed by Diogenes in *Lives and Opinions of Eminent Philosophers*.

[15] As explained on p.73 of *The Complete Stanislavsky Toolkit*, Bella Merlin (Nick Hern Books: 2014).

So, want something. Understand why you want it. Understand how you might get it. Think about what might stand in your way.

Your desires make you credible. In my experience, senior business people tend to be ambitious. Desire is authentic.

Be Funny

I said to my wife the other night, "Did you ever in your wildest dreams think that I would be writing a book about PR?"

There was a long and significant pause.

"Honey," she replied. "You're not in my wildest dreams!"

That's an adapted version of the joke used by marketing specialist, author and venture capitalist Guy Kawasaki to open his TEDx talk.[16] It got a big laugh on the day, and I'm sure it's been tickling some of his other audiences for a while.

There is no better weapon than humour for those individuals and businesses that want to cut through and be noticed. But attempting gags is sometimes perceived as a risky business.

The easiest route to humour is a little bit of self-mocking humility. Not too much, just a flavour of vulnerability. If anyone is the butt of the joke, it should probably be you.

Stand-up comedians spend their lives in front of (sometimes hostile) audiences. They hone their material and delivery through years of practise. They test jokes obsessively and constantly refine and adapt their material.

What can business leaders learn from the professional joke merchants?

In his excellent book *Do You Talk Funny?* David Nihill decided to overcome his fear of public speaking by pretending to be an accomplished comedian called 'Irish Dave' for a full year. He crashed every comedy club, festival and show he could find.

This masochism strategy gave Nihill a firm belief that *anyone* can be funny, as long as you focus on simple, everyday stories. These stories may illustrate the absurdity and frustrations of life but on a bigger scale. The humour comes from the details and unexpected juxtapositions.

The classic joke formula has a lead-in (the set up), followed by anticipation (often just a timely pause), followed by the punchline. The reason we laugh is that the punchline is something different to what we were expecting. We've been taken in one direction and then spun into another one:

---

[16] Guy Kawasaki speaking to TEDxBerkeley: www.youtube.com/watch?v=Mtjatz9r-Vc

Q: What's the best way to make a small fortune on the stock market?

A: Start off with a big fortune.

And so on.

Some business people I've met react strongly against the very idea of humour. They want to be serious, professional, capable leaders. Jokes? Leave those to the after-dinner speaker we've hired in.

Or they say, "Fine, could you write me a couple of jokes?"

I think both approaches are a mistake.

Business people shouldn't try to be something they're not. The type of jokes that work for Michael McIntyre would bomb at the annual results presentation. But business people can almost always be a lighter, funnier, more spontaneous version of themselves.

One of the best guests I've had on my *PR for Humans* podcast is comedian, broadcaster and public speaker Mark Dolan. He told me that 'humour' is too abstract a thing to aim for. Instead, you should aim to be a bigger, slightly crazier version of yourself... maybe with a little twist.

"I've never met a human being that doesn't employ humour in their lives," Mark said. "I've almost never met a human being that doesn't employ humour in the workplace. Even the driest characters have some wit."

The secret, according to Mark, is to be open to improvising. You can break the ice with a casual moment – that little reference to the lavish catering or the size of the stage may be enough to get a laugh, if it's 'in the moment'.

Communication is a live experience. The magic often lies in the unexpected. Perhaps someone drops a glass and you say, "Can you just calm down a little on table three?" Or the PowerPoint goes down and you say, "This keeps happening to me. My ideas keep breaking the internet."

These lines are not massively funny on the page. But live, in the moment, the bar for humour is much lower. They could well get a big laugh.

In the desperately dry world of business, we are all desperate for a chuckle. The audience is on your side. They want a few jokes, or failing that, some lighter moments.

Be the Coach

Leadership communication is often about drawing things out of others, rather than transmitting information about yourself. There's great power in being the person who gets people to think and find answers, rather than telling them what to do.

This goes back to the idea that runs through this whole book: it's as much about the human audience as it is about you, the human being. Great communicators are often the coaches rather than the managers. The coach of a football team must bring the best out of the players, ask questions of them, but be clear that it's up to them to supply the answers.

In my field, I see a fundamental difference between coaching and training. They seem to be interchangeable terms. Media coach, media trainer. Fitness coach, fitness trainer. What's the difference? I think it's a question of where you put the focus. With a *trainer*, the focus is on the person delivering the training. They are there to pass on information and get the trainee to perform within a prescribed framework of activity. The job of the *coach*, however, is to unlock an individual's existing potential to maximise their performance.

Coaching helps a person to find their own answers, rather than telling them what to do. The focus is on the audience rather than the speaker. As a leader and a communicator, you are trying to forge a connection with an audience by drawing something out of them.

Proponents of the coaching method – like the late Sir John Whitmore, author of the industry manual *Coaching for Performance* – believe we all have the innate ability to teach ourselves, but we need a coach to steer us in the right direction by asking us questions.

Rather than sitting someone down and transmitting information at them, coaches operate in listening mode. Often, the subject knows deep down what the problem is and, with some guidance, can find the most effective route for themselves.

The trick for the coach is always to ask open questions. Often these are the simple 'what' and 'how' questions:

- *What* would you like to achieve?
- *What* is the real challenge here?
- *How* do you think success could be measured?
- *How* will you know when you've reached your objectives?

I find that when I approach 'media training' with a coaching mindset, the results are more powerful because I'm asking the individual to construct their own agenda, set of personal priorities and plan to reach them. As the specialist, I can guide (and even sometimes teach), but only once the person I'm coaching engages with his or her own goals.

Most 'training' is forgotten within a few weeks. But 'coaching' can produce lasting, more powerful results because the participant has helped to build a solution to their own set of problems.

As a former reporter, I like asking questions. The questions must be neutral and not in any way loaded. As the interviewer-coach, I can get the business executive to relax, open up a bit and communicate more honestly and powerfully.

I've come to believe that the coaching mindset is critical in PR, both for comms advisers and business leaders. The adviser who can carefully ask clients the right questions to reveal the *real* goals, challenges, obstacles and opportunities will be much more effective than the consultant who marches into the room and starts telling people what to do.

So, go from transmitting mode to listening mode. Ask questions and really think about the answers.

The professional services firm EY launched a good campaign in 2016 about asking better questions.[17] Each blog, video and report they released started with a question: 'Is selling the new buying?', 'Can you prepare for a future you can't predict?', 'What does purpose mean for public policy?' and so on.

I think this gave out the impression of a clever firm, prepared to ask ever more probing questions in the search for the right answers. This is more interesting and more appealing than the usual 'thought leadership', which often starts with the answer and assembles a pile of 'evidence' to try to back it up.

Genuine communicators seek to *stimulate* thought, not to prescribe it too rigidly.

This is reflected in the media context we now operate in, which has gone from transmitting information (broadcasting) to interacting with our audiences (social media).

Information must flow both ways or companies and individuals can easily seem remote and out of touch. Questions create good conversations. To ask the right questions, we must summon our inner coach.

That's as important for the CEO as it is for the new graduate on their first day in the office.

Listen

The best coaches are the best communicators. They are also the best listeners.

People love talking about themselves. Successful business people *really* love talking about themselves. Their all-time favourite subject is how they

17 EY Better Questions Campaign: www.ey.com/gl/en/about-us/our-global-approach/global-review/global-review-2016-asking-better-questions

got to the lofty position they currently occupy. They enjoy nothing more than describing the brilliant decisions they made along the way, and how they overcame every obstacle.

This may or may not be incredibly dull, depending on their natural ability as a storyteller. Before helping these people to find a better, more engaging story, people like me often need to close our mouths and open our ears.

The best piece of advice I got when crossing over from journalism to public relations was this: *good operators listen*. The temptation to switch immediately into transmitting mode is powerful, especially when the problems seem blindingly obvious. We must, however, not just bite our tongues but often hold them clamped between our teeth for several minutes – maybe up to an hour.

Our task is often to find the problem – the *real* problem – which may be very different from the brief that has been sent out, or the agenda that was drawn up ahead of the meeting. We can't come up with answers until we understand the issue. We can't find a better story until we've first heard the *prevailing version* of the story.

The listening habit needs to be cultivated. As Dale Carnegie wrote in his seminal *How to Win Friends and Influence People*, human beings want, above all else, to feel important. They want others to perceive their lives and their businesses as significant. If we go into a room and talk *at* people, we will be thought of as boring. If we lecture people on the first meeting, we will likely not be invited back.

If, however, we sit down with the main intention of listening, we will win trust. Our host will feel, rightly, significant in their own domain. We will tease out a much clearer picture of the situation. We will get closer to the real problem. All the while, we will be buying ourselves some time. Our brains can be whirring away silently, waiting for the moment when the host turns to us after a rambling 45 minutes and says, "What do *you* think?"

Then we can flick the switch. We can move from being the listener/questioner to being the transmitter. This is when we start to map out the solution to the problem. Time and again, whether in a formal pitch, a 'chemistry' meeting or a kick-off session, I've seen the switch being flicked too soon. Those doing the pitching launch into the answer before the question or context has been defined. This puts the customer on the defensive, shows a lack of respect and erodes the very thing you are trying to establish: trust.

Don't worry about being brilliant or cracking the problem quickly. Instead, concentrate on listening hard, joining the dots in your own mind and nudging your target in roughly the right direction with your questions. In fact, a brilliant result is when the customer/partner/employee, in the end, comes up with the answer themselves, and thanks you for it.

Pause

One of the most effective ways to communicate is to stop talking. For a second, for a minute or even for an hour.

There are many reasons why those in business should understand the power of the pause.

A pause gives you time to think, to breathe and to compose your next remark. When an audience sees someone who's comfortable with a pause, they see a thinker. They see a listener. They see someone who responds to those around them.

When I used to edit radio features for the BBC's *Today Programme* or World Service Radio, the temptation would be to cram in as much as possible: background effects, music, interview clips, voiceover links. Every split second of the package was stuffed with sound. Then one day a producer gave me one of the best pieces of advice I ever received as a broadcaster: "Let it breathe."

Loosen the edits. Take out the distractions. Lengthen the clips. Slow it down. Do more with less.

If we let it breathe, we can *hear* the thoughts and connect with them on a deeper level. If someone says something meaningful, we can allow a second or two for the idea to sink in properly. If someone doesn't immediately know the answer to a question, we don't mind if they pause and spend a moment trying to figure it out. These are human qualities that will enhance, not hinder, your communication.

Some inexperienced broadcasters hate this. They call any silences 'dead air' and try to push noise into them. But one of the reasons podcasts are successful is that, because the interviews are longer, less produced and less packaged, we can *hear* the thinking. We can get to know people with all their flaws. And because they are imperfect and less polished, we trust them more. The power comes from authenticity.

In a speech, an interview or a board meeting, slow down and don't feel the need to jump in and fill every silence with sentences. In conversations and meetings, we aren't just presenting at each other, we are trying to share thoughts. To think, we need to let it breathe.

As an interviewer, I try to hold back as much as possible and listen to people talk before charging in with my opinions. If there are silences, that's not only fine, it's good.

You need to feel comfortable with silence. Let the silence do the work, because something magical happens when you use the power of the pause. Someone will quickly seek to fill it with something, and that's when you can uncover a new angle or extract some new meaning from a person or situation.

When I was interviewing politicians at Westminster, I would often do this: allow them to parrot their key message or line for the day, and then deliberately leave a pause. Because they weren't comfortable with silence, they would usually go on to say something more interesting and newsworthy than their original utterance. Good for me. Not always good for them.

In an interview, deliver your big thought, then pause. In a speech, pause before and after the bit you really want the audience to remember.

Pause at the beginning of meetings. Pause before you begin summing up:

"OK, let me summarise the situation."

Stop. Count 1, 2, 3, 4, 5.

"Here's what I think we should do..."

Power.

In a world of constant chatter and distraction, silence is special.

In silence, we can also start to imagine a picture of what has just been said. We can, in our minds, create IMAGERY, which is the final principle of *PR for Humans*.

Summary

- **Humility gives you power:** You might think that showing any weakness or vulnerability compromises your communication. If anything, it does the opposite. Tell stories about failure, but also display an almost fanatical desire to learn from mistakes. And you must *want* something. That is a human desire we all recognise.

- **Solve the Storyteller's Paradox:** The story has got to be about you, but it can't be all about you. If you list only great things you've done and wonderful achievements, the audience will switch off and suspect you. It's your story, but the act of telling it is more about the audience than you.

- **Talk less, listen more:** Adopt a coaching mindset. Bring the best out of others by asking questions. Be a seeker of answers and a problem-solver. Sometimes, just stop talking and use the power of the pause. Humans respond to *listeners* as much as, if not more than, *talkers*.

8. IMAGERY

In the final chapter of Part 1, we will look at the power of IMAGERY in leadership communications. We'll see why leaders need to master metaphor, create visual 'moments' and find pictures to explain numbers and sequences.

Use Metaphor

Practitioners of *PR for Humans* must be visual thinkers, even if they mostly communicate with words and numbers.

Ten years ago, at the height of the financial crisis, the world was introduced to a highly technical and obscure process called quantitative easing (QE). In short, it meant that the world's central banks could create money out of thin air and blast huge clouds of it into the economy to avert recession.

Around this time, the chief executive of one of Britain's largest banks was invited to the BBC to give a briefing to our team in the Business Unit. He spoke for about 45 minutes and I've now forgotten everything he said. Everything, that is, except one remark. He was asked about QE.

"QE," he said, "is *like a flamethrower* – be careful whose hands you put it in."

Those words stuck in my head long after everything else had gone. Why? Because he used a powerful metaphor. I was reminded of this story a couple of years ago when a former senior official at the UK Treasury was tweeting about the same subject:

> *QE like heroin: need ever increasing fixes to create a high. Meanwhile, negative side effects increase. Time to move on.*[18]

These remarks were reported all over the business press. The metaphor gave power to the opinion and made it immediately accessible and memorable.

Metaphors, like many of the best communication ideas, originated in ancient Greece. Aristotle said that being good at metaphor is by far the

---

[18] Tweet from former Treasury official Nick Macpherson: @nickmacpherson2, 21 August 2017.

most important gift for any writer. The concept comes from the Greek word *metaphora*, meaning a 'transfer'. When we are using a metaphor, we are transferring one meaning onto another.

Metaphors are most useful when we take a non-visual concept (like QE) and make it highly visual. Processing words and analysis takes effort, but our brains love pictures. We can enjoy images all day long. Anything that lights up the 'mind's eye' will be remembered long after solid analysis and numbers have been forgotten.

I was introduced to the power of metaphor on a speechwriting course run by Simon Lancaster, author of the excellent *Speech Writing: The Expert Guide*. Lancaster is well schooled in political use of metaphor.

Let's just look at a few metaphors used by British prime ministers:

- Winston Churchill: "From Stettin in the Baltic to Trieste in the Adriatic, **an** *iron curtain* has descended across the continent."[19]
- Harold Macmillan: "**The** *wind of change* is blowing through this continent. Whether we like it or not this growth of national consciousness is a political fact."[20]
- Harold Wilson: "The Britain that is going to be forged in **the** *white heat* of this revolution will be no place for restrictive practises or for outdated methods on either side of industry."[21]
- Margaret Thatcher: "You *turn* if you want to. The Lady's not for *turning*."[22]
- *Tony Blair:* "I can only go one way, **I've not got a** *reverse gear.*"[23]

But be warned: metaphors can sometimes be too direct and powerful. If you give your audience a great metaphor, it will be quoted and remembered, so make sure the image is spot on and reflects the argument you really want to make.

Some metaphors – particularly sporting or weather metaphors – are tired and overused. These could be an 'open goal' for your critics and create 'headwinds' for you.

Other metaphors – of disease, pestilence, war, conflict, excretion and so on – can create strong emotional reactions. These are best avoided, unless you seek to arouse those negative feelings.

---

[19] Speech by Winston Churchill at Westminster College, Missouri, 5 March 1946.
[20] Speech by UK prime minister Harold Macmillan to the Parliament of South Africa, 3 February 1960.
[21] Speech by Labour leader Harold Wilson to Labour Party Conference, 1 October 1963.
[22] Speech by Conservative prime minister Margaret Thatcher to Conservative Party Conference, 10 October 1980.
[23] Speech by Labour prime minister Tony Blair to the Labour Party Conference, 30 September 2003.

Some metaphors can be powerful but horrible. One of the charts that financial analysts sometimes reference is called the 'vomiting camel' graph. It shows a volatile decline in prices. The image is nothing special in the financial markets, just a jittery decline in value, but the 'sick' metaphor gives it an unpleasant stickiness.

George Orwell's advice was never to use a metaphor or simile that you are used to seeing in print. Of course, if journalists followed this advice, most newspaper headlines and articles would never be written!

Most metaphors are borrowed or adapted, but the best ones are original (enough). They are the sniffer dogs of communication, finding their way to exactly the person you want to reach. If you don't do that with spoken or written metaphors, you might instead use real images and illustrations.

Use Words, but Think in Pictures

When I was a television news reporter, I would have to find ways each day to match up three things: the story, the pictures and the script.

The first questions are always: what is the story we're trying to tell here? What is the headline? Who is the main character? What have they done or not done?

The next question is: What fresh shots do we have to illustrate it? Good pictures support the story. Much of the time, however, the shots that are available don't quite fit what we're trying to say, or the pictures are so powerful that they unbalance the report and distract from the main arguments.

Once we have decided what the story is, and think we have the pictures to match, we then try to arrange them into sequences – collections of images that make sense. The sequences must fit together into a report that might only be 1 minute 45 seconds or 2 minutes in duration.

You can write the script as you edit each sequence, or edit the sequences and then write a script to fit, or write a script and then find video to match. In TV news, the power comes from the symbiosis of writing and pictures – the best results usually occur when you are working closely with a skilful editor who is cutting the sequences.

In business communication, I'm often surprised by the separation of written and visual communication. A text-heavy document might be produced, which is then sent to someone else to turn into a set of slides. Someone else is then asked to create an edited video. A completely different team or individual might be asked to create a sequence of infographics.

In a world of email overload, it's very easy to lose the visual elements of a story. Versions of documents fly backward and forward between departments or between agencies and clients. Only at the very end does the 'creative' person come along and try to make it visual.

To be more successful with our communication, we should think in pictures from the beginning.

When you are standing up to deliver a speech or approach a media interview, you need to decide not just what you want to say, but how you want the audience to see it in their mind's eye. It is the ability that humans possess to imagine, to visualise, that gives our best storytelling its immense power to move and to motivate.

Visual storytelling preceded written storytelling by tens of thousands of years. Throughout recorded history – from drawings on cave walls, to Roman mosaics, to the Bayeux Tapestry, to Renaissance painting, to modern comics and Instagram posts – we've used pictures to tell stories. The best communicators *must* be able to think in pictures. This isn't just about creating a 'photo op' or a nice logo to stick on the front of the report – it's about combining words and images skilfully to conjure abstract ideas into life. Sometimes with metaphor. Sometimes by vivid description.

Children's illustrator and storyteller Marcia Williams is one of the best visual storytellers around. She has produced around 60 wonderful books, which take quite complicated stories and subjects – like the Egyptians, Greek myths, the Romans, Chaucer, Shakespeare, the First World War – and reimagine them as visual storybooks for children. When I met her at her home in London to record an episode of my podcast, she gave me this insight into her storytelling process:

> The hardest part is getting started. Every story has its own needs and wants and has to be told in a certain way. The hardest bit is finding the voice for the story. The writing always comes first, because everything hangs on that. I can then enrich the story with pictures and make complicated things clearer with pictures.

This is very interesting. I had half expected her to tell me that she starts by sketching the pictures and then writes the text below to describe the images. But that's not visual storytelling. The words should complement but not replicate the visual content (see my section in Part 2, Chapter 2 on PowerPoint!).

This is *not* a process of excessive simplification or reducing a story to its simplest constituent parts. Marcia Williams told me that audiences –

including and especially children – hate being patronised. "There's a huge difference," she said, "between making something accessible and dumbing it down."

Good pictures can allow a writer to convey *even more* information, humour, subtlety and nuance than words alone. But only if they are well designed within a clear story framework.

Single images, whether put on slides or posted on social media, might provoke a knee-jerk response and generate 'likes' or superficial 'engagement'. The real power, though, comes when visual sequences connect into meaningful stories. They allow you to *make the complex accessible*.

If you want to do *PR for Humans* well, if you want to reach audiences more powerfully, use words – but always try to think of communication, ultimately, as a sequence of pictures. If a speech divides into seven chunks, challenge yourself to imagine a single image for each section. If you're writing a blog, think of an image that you'd like to plant in the reader's mind.

Storyboard your business and your life. Try to think of it as a comic strip – of scenes, moments and characters.

Use Numbers Imaginatively

When I applied to be an economics correspondent, part of the interview process involved a numerical storytelling test. Each candidate was given a large table of figures which might show the UK's trading position, projected budget surplus or something else to do with consumer spending or business investment.

The challenge was to find the story in the numbers. What did all the millions and billions and percentages show? What did they tell us about the economy? How could we make those numbers relevant and interesting to the millions of people who switched on the TV news?

Under the interview spotlight, the table of hundreds of pieces of data becomes a blurry, confusing and chaotic mess. But somewhere lurking in this data is the important story of the day. It might well be a story that nobody else has spotted, or that government press officers are steering you away from in favour of something more positive.

The language of business is the language of numbers. Whether it's the government's budget, the company's annual results or the latest advertising metrics, leaders must somehow find ways to use numbers to win arguments, build support and ultimately enhance reputation.

One of Britain's foremost number wizards is Marcus du Sautoy, Professor for the Public Understanding of Science at Oxford University, keynote speaker and star of numerous TV shows about maths and science. He has spent his life looking for the meaning in numbers – the codes that unlock our understanding of the world.

"A mathematician is at heart a pattern-searcher," he told me on the *PR for Humans* podcast. "That's what they are trying to do: look at the patterns underlying the chaos and mess around us. If we understand those patterns in the past, we can read into the future."

But, as Marcus explained, predicting the future is incredibly difficult in complex and chaotic systems like the economy. The tiniest changes can have a massive influence on where we end up. This is the famous idea of the butterfly's wings beating on one side of the world and causing a hurricane on the other. And yet, from the Bank of England, to the Treasury, to the leading investment companies, every economic organisation is desperately – and unsuccessfully – trying to forecast the future.

Nobody in business or politics wants to stand up and say, "Sorry folks, we just don't know what next year will bring", or "Trust me, this is the right decision, but I have no idea what the outcome will actually be". We want and expect our leaders to see enough of a good future to be able to guide us there. I do, though, think credibility is enhanced when the degree of uncertainty (for the range of possible outcomes) is sometimes acknowledged.

The core problem, however, is that audiences, populations and voters are easily confused by numbers. They like the idea of certainty, even when the reality is uncertain.

As Marcus du Sautoy told me: "The human has a very bad intuition for large numbers and large data sets. That is why we often get misled... humans didn't get exposed in an evolutionary way to a large number of cases. A 'million' or a 'billion' is kind of like infinite for us – we have no intuition for it."

Business leaders hoping to project their messages with clarity and impact need to think about numbers carefully. A list of millions and billions and percentages will be useful for professional analysts poring over the data sets and crunching their calculations, but most of us need a confidently told story about what it all means.

When presenting the annual results or the pitch for the big investment, think about the story you want to tell and then choose numbers carefully to illustrate the story – only one number for each point.

The old rule is that you should use round numbers to make things clearer, but as presidential speechwriter James C. Humes points out in his book *Speak Like Churchill, Stand Like Lincoln*, there is sometimes a trade-off between memorability and credibility.

Take these two statements:

- "We've attracted 10,000 customers this year".
- "We've added 9,958 customers this year. 9,958 more people now using this service. Each one as valued as the other".

The first statement is more memorable, but the second is more credible.

There are times in your professional life when you can sacrifice the round number for the exact number, if you want to give the impression of rigour and accuracy. At other times, you may want to present yourself as the big-picture leader, unfussed by the exact detail.

Too many numbers, delivered as a list, will always numb and confuse an audience. Yes, we want proof and numerical 'evidence', but in small doses. When using numbers, try to make them visual and give them a scale that people can understand:

- "It's the equivalent of £25 for every household in London".
- "That's the amount of energy needed to power a city the size of Berlin for a year".

In a memorable speech in 1958, President Eisenhower said this:

> To understand the billion-dollar deficit, imagine taking all the one-dollar bills in a billion and laying them out end to end. Why, it would more than go to the moon and back again!

We can all visualise that.

Create Moments

Reputation is shaped by memory. And memory is fuzzy and emotion-soaked.

We are not able to know or recall everything that a person or business has done and then decide whether we like that person or business. Instead, we form a general impression based on a few key moments that we *can* remember. These will then be rapidly averaged into an imperfect judgement. Once lodged, impressions based on a small number of events or episodes can be hard to change.

In their book *The Power of Moments* Chip and Dan Heath investigate these ideas. They ask: why do we remember certain things and forget others?

When we assess our experiences and draw our conclusions (about a product, an experience, a service or a person), we don't average minute-by-minute sensations. Instead we remember the standout moments: the highs, the lows and the big shifts.

Look back on your life. You can see it like an edited movie trailer. You can see, and *feel*, those big moments: graduation, first kiss, first job, birth of a child. You can picture the best and the worst scenes. You can remember the smells and the sounds.

Now think at random of any individual you know who is not a member of your close family or one of your dearest friends. Think about whether you like them, respect them, suspect them or dislike them. Now ask: how many data points am I using to make that decision? It's likely that their reputation (in your eyes) will be based on a small number of moments.

Now think about a place (maybe a restaurant or a hotel) you've visited a few times. Can you remember anything special that happened? Did someone go out of their way to deliver exceptional service? Did someone do something that was rude or offensive? Strikingly good or shockingly bad, snapshots are lodged in our decision bank.

Visualise them.

We tend to live our lives, and run our businesses, as if every minute is equal to every other minute. There's often little to distinguish one week from the next. We plough on, imagining that we can succeed by squeezing more into every hour. In doing so, we are not investing in the potential of *moments* to deliver results.

When we reach back into our memories, we see the moments that peak above the ordinary, that shift our understanding of the world, that capture our love and excitement and in which we make powerful new connections. So, let us seek to create them.

The story of your life. The story of your business. Tell that story by thinking of the key moments – those times that were in some way exceptional.

When writing your speeches and articles, ask yourself this: am I doing or saying anything here which anyone in my audience will consider a key moment? Will they remember one thing that excited them or shifted their perception in some way? Because in a few weeks or months, the lists and numbers and analysis will be forgotten. Anyone who heard you or read your work will be left with a general impression of the way you made them feel.

Those in PR have always tried to be the creators of moments: the events, the stunts, the launches. The best practitioners find ways of reimagining these things, being memorable and meaningful without being crass and silly. It's not easy.

Like so much in *PR for Humans*, less is more.

Look ahead to the annual conference, the big charity dinner, the launch of the next deal or the day you welcome new graduates into your organisation. Decide how to make it special. Shape it into a moment – a visual memory – that those attending will never forget.

Summary

- **Use metaphor:** Metaphors are the sniffer dogs of communication. They are powerful ways to convey your ideas and opinions. Many, however, are tired. Find original ones.

- **Think in pictures:** Paint pictures with your words. Human communication is visual, even when using words and numbers. If you are talking about someone, describe them. If you are telling a story, bring it to life visually with specific details. If you are using numbers, make them real and relevant.

- **Create visual moments and memories:** If you want to create an impact, think about how to create big moments that spike the excitement. Make the speech more memorable by making it visual. Find one exciting thing that makes this point in time special.

PART 2

Telling Your Story
Techniques

1. SPEECHES

In the second half of this book, we'll see how the principles from Part 1 can be applied in the real situations leaders find themselves in.

Belief. Clarity. Opinion. Energy. Context. Time. Humility. Imagery.

These principles don't change, whether you are delivering a speech, doing a media interview, making a video or writing a blog.

These are the principles leaders need to master. Applying these principles is what I call PR for Humans. So let's see how we can put them to work, starting with the crunch moment for so many in business: the speech.

In this chapter, we'll see why a speech needs to be personal and have a clear argument. We'll look at some ways to begin and end speeches. We will also see how we can apply some of our principles to other aspects of public speaking, like pitches and panel events.

Make It Personal

The best speeches are personal. They show the character of the speaker. The first thing we need to do when preparing a speech, I believe, is to look inwards.

What do we care about? What bothers us? What makes us emotional? What makes us excited? How can we use our own story to convey an idea? Which moments of our lives were meaningful and important?

Some of the best speeches I've helped to craft have been very simple. The speaker has told a few stories, related them to a theme and made it all very personal, often mentioning certain individuals in the audience who have been part of those stories, thus demonstrating humility as well.

It's so easy to overcomplicate a speech. To lose the character and personality of the speaker. To lose the audience by failing to involve them.

Make it personal. Do that first. Then prepare your argument.

Find an Argument

You often need a topic for your speech. A topic isn't just a theme; it's where you construct your argument. Good speeches often make a case. They try to convince someone of something. To inspire, we must persuade. To persuade, we must win the argument.

It sounds obvious, but the argument has got be clear and *arguable*. You should be able to imagine someone standing up and making a counter-argument. You must have something or someone to argue against.

In the ancient Roman Republic, the skills of rhetoric were developed by lawyers, who were also powerful politicians. They acted as prosecutors and defence barristers for wealthy citizens accused of crimes. They took a stand on behalf of an individual. They were fierce competitors. They built their careers on winning arguments. The most famous of them was Marcus Cicero.

Cicero used the law courts to build a reputation as the best speaker in Rome, and one of the greatest orators in history. With every victory in the cases he prosecuted and defended, he moved closer to becoming consul, the highest elected position in the Republic.

Every speech, said Cicero, needs a topic:

> A topic is the seat of an argument, and an argument is a reason which causes men to believe a thing which would otherwise be doubtful.[24]

'The seat of an argument'. I love Cicero's metaphor here. Think about this when preparing a speech. The topic we choose must be something that we can *sit* an argument on. The thing we argue gets our audience to believe something *which would otherwise be doubtful*.

Good speeches change audiences. If a speech tells an audience something they already believe, it is pointless. A speech can *persuade* us of something to which there can be legitimate and logical opposition. Take this example of a speech title:

'We must innovate to succeed'

It is a poor title, because there is nothing to sit an argument on. No intelligent person can really disagree with that. And yet so many business speeches follow this formula. There is no tension. There is no debate. There is no opinion. It doesn't take a specific enough position. As a member of the audience, I can't be inspired because I can't be persuaded.

Now look at this example:

'The threat to jobs from Artificial Intelligence has been overstated'

Ah ha! Now we are in business. There is an argument here. How do we know? Because we can imagine being in the audience and disagreeing with the statement. I might even be able to get up and argue that the threat from AI has been *under*stated.

---

24 Marcus Tullius Cicero, *The Orations*, Volume IV.

Now take this example:

'We need to do 7 things this year to succeed'

Again, this isn't a great title. The speech will be a list. It's fine as far as it goes – a lot of business speeches follow this sort of a structure, a list of five or seven things that need to happen to drive results – but there is no topic. Cicero would say, "There is no seat for my argument!"

Now consider this title:

'The single most important thing we need to do this year is X'

This is better. We are getting specific and taking a position. We can imagine being in the audience and disagreeing, thinking that something else should be the top priority this year. It's closer to a proper argument.

It's no coincidence that many parliamentarians are former lawyers. They are used to arguing a case, having a position, making a stand. Almost every decent political speech will take a side in a debate. You take a side by having an opinion, and having an opinion gets you noticed – as we discovered in Part 1.

The temptation when delivering a speech is to try to position yourself in the mid-point of the spectrum of audience opinions. That's the safe option. You simply reflect where your audience already is. You hold up a mirror to them. They feel comfortable. Nobody throws any tomatoes. But nobody feels, in any way, excited or changed.

The speaker needs to *move* you. They must shift your position, challenge your assumptions and take you to a new place. They often do this by setting out, and hopefully winning, an argument.

The best speeches can also surprise. They argue something unexpected or intriguing. They challenge us to think differently. They move us. They persuade us.

You don't need a big argument for every meeting and every team talk, but if you are invited to speak at more significant 'town hall' events, or to deliver keynote speeches, challenge yourself to come up with one. Your argument will become the headline for your speech. It will give you the golden thread that runs all the way through the speech. This is clarity. This is good communication.

As well as convincing and persuading, speeches can also move an audience in another way, by giving them something new – a way of looking at the world or understanding life that they hadn't considered before.

This is the power of an idea.

Put TED to Bed

These days, when we think of speeches built around an idea, we think of the now ubiquitous TED-style talk. Named after the TED (Technology, Entertainment and Design) Conference, which has been held annually since 1990, these are 18–20-minute speeches built around one concept. TED talks are designed to be clear and accessible, but also challenging. The point is to get the audience to think about an issue in a new and interesting way.

Some of these talks have been watched millions of times online. Whole books (lots of them!) have been written deconstructing the formula of TED's success. Now, when I meet clients, they sometimes ask whether I can help them deliver TED talks. The answer is: yes, kind of. Not actual TED talks, usually. They are quite difficult to secure. But, sure, I can tell you what's going on in a successful TED talk, and help you learn some of the lessons.

I'm a big admirer of TED talks. However, I also like to point out some of their difficulties, particularly when business people try to copy the formula. Here's my view:

- TED talks are about the power of a single idea. You need to have one thing. It's got to be a challenging and unusual take on something that matters. TED-style talks need to feel important. In business, you may have one thing – one big idea – that is different and that you *really* want to share. In my experience, most people in business don't have one thing, or at least they don't have it *yet*, so a TED-style talk may not be appropriate.
- The best TED talks are emotional and personal. The speaker needs to open up. They need to bring a *lot* of themselves to the show. They need to feel completely comfortable telling revealing stories about their lives and their journey. Great if you can do it, but for lots of people out there, going full TED may not be comfortable.
- TED talks are highly produced. It may look like the speaker is just coming out with this brilliant material on the platform, but that is not the case. They spend weeks and often months honing the idea, rewriting drafts, rehearsing obsessively. Often, they memorise the entire speech, or at the very least learn every minute transition. The talks are then set on stages that look casual but have been very carefully designed. The whole thing is shot from multiple camera angles to look as polished as a live speech can ever be.

- TED-style talks are not good places either to impart lots of information or to win a contentious 'political' argument. You need to be the starry-eyed optimist giving the audience hope, or opening their eyes to something important/magical, but ultimately uncontroversial.
- TED-talkers stand on a red circle and seem to talk without notes. In fact, there are often different forms of prompts and cue cards available. Someone who has grown comfortable delivering podium speeches will have to do a lot of coaching on posture, body language and voice to look at ease on the TED-style platform.

So, do you still want to deliver a TED-type talk? Great. Let's do it. But a word of warning: getting all of the above in place may take a while. A few weeks at least.

For everyone else, it's OK to put TED to bed. For now. We can wake him up when and if you are ready.

But here's what we can take from the whole TED experience that you can use in *any* speech:

- Care about the material. If it matters to you, it will matter to the audience.
- Be disciplined on timings. 18 minutes is a long speech, in my view. Go longer than TED and your ratings will suffer.
- Use stories. Find experiences from your own life that illuminate the subject you are speaking about. Make it as personal as you can manage.
- Find real clarity about your argument. A TED talk is never a list of five things or seven things. It has one headline. Yours must too. Even if you don't have one big idea to change the world, you need to be able to sum up your talk in a simple sentence.

Look back at the principles in the first half of this book:
Belief. Clarity. Opinion. Energy. Context. Time. Humility. Imagery.

Think: how can I bring those principles into my speeches? They will certainly take you in the direction of some of the better TED-talkers. But, ultimately, you must decide how far *you* want to go.

Whatever anyone else is doing – on TED stages or anywhere else – *you've* got to decide what type of speaker you want to be. If you are comfortable, the audience will be too.

Start Strong

At the beginning of your talk, you need to give the audience some drugs.

That's the view of Simon Lancaster, one of the UK's leading speechwriters and communication experts.

No, not real drugs, silly. Here's Simon on the *PR for Humans* podcast:

> You need to get the audience high. If you want to make people smile, tell them a joke and get the dopamine flowing. If you want people to feel sad or emotionally connected to you, then tell them a story and you'll get the oxytocin flowing. If you want to make them feel alert, then ask them a really challenging question that they did not see coming and that will get the cortisol going. It's all about the drugs!

The beginning of a speech is the most important bit. A speaker has just seconds (a minute or two at most) to get the audience on side and convince them that this is going to be worth listening to.

Let's look quickly at some examples:

Joke
Mark Weinberger, CEO of the professional services firm EY, giving a speech to a diversity conference in 2014, said:

> It's great to see everyone – good morning. With that introduction... I can't wait to hear what I have to say.[25]

Simple. Funny enough. Self-deprecating. The audience immediately likes this guy.

Story
This is how the writer Susan Cain began her talk on the power of introverts in 2012:

> When I was nine years old, I went off to summer camp for the first time. And my mother packed me a suitcase full of books... in my family, reading was the primary group activity... You have the animal warmth of your family sitting right next to you, but you are also free to go roaming around the adventureland inside your own mind.[26]

There is no "I am honoured to be speaking here tonight, and I want to start by thanking..." No. Cain goes straight into the story, which establishes

---

[25] CEO of EY Mark Weinberger's diversity speech: www.youtube.com/watch?v=5xLJBHVDYlI
[26] Susan Cain, TED talk: www.ted.com/talks/susan_cain_the_power_of_introverts

an emotional connection to the subject, and to the audience. The oxytocin is definitely flowing.

Question

Simon Sinek, author and motivational speaker, built his career on a single question: why? By asking why a company exists, you uncover its core purpose. Its real reason for being. He began his much-viewed 2009 talk with a series of questions:

> How do you explain when things don't go as we assume? Or better, how do you explain when others are able to achieve things that seem to defy all of the assumptions? For example: Why is Apple so innovative? Year after year, after year, they're more innovative than all their competition. And yet, they're just a computer company.[27]

If you ask a big question at the beginning of a speech then the rest of the talk must provide the answer. You need to show, by the end, that you've solved the problem.

Statistic

You might like to deploy a big/shocking statistic. TV chef Jamie Oliver did this in his talk on obesity in 2010:

> Sadly, in the next 18 minutes when I do our chat, four Americans that are alive will be dead through the food that they eat.[28]

This statistic is memorable and unsettling for the audience, who are immediately gripped by Oliver's message about better nutrition and better ingredients.

Statement of intent

There's also the possibility of opening with a big statement of intent:

- "Our ambition is to be the best in the world at IT".
- "By this time next year, we're going to double sales".
- "Staff retention is the biggest problem we face – this is how we're going to crack it".

---

[27] Simon Sinek, TED talk: www.ted.com/talks/simon_sinek_how_great_leaders_inspire_action
[28] Jamie Oliver, TED talk: www.ted.com/talks/jamie_oliver

The bold, purposeful beginning allows you to take on the mantle of action. Immediately this message goes out to the audience: this person isn't messing around.

Topical reference

You could mention something that's happened in the news that day, or make a remark about the location where the event is happening. This gives your talk those priceless qualities of spontaneity and relevance.

Most speeches would benefit from getting to the hook faster. Don't fill the beginning of your talk with platitudes, waffle, context, health and safety announcements and to-do lists. Tell the audience what the point of the talk is.

In those early moments of the speech, do everything you can to make the audience feel special and bring them to attention. Maybe you could ask for a show of hands. Maybe you could put up a puzzling image on a slide and ask them to guess what it is. Maybe you could pick out one or two individuals in the audience who you particularly admire.

Find the drug that works for you. Then administer it quickly.

Finish Stronger

Many years ago, I was taking part in an undergraduate public speaking competition. The speech went well. I'd made the crusty old fellows in the audience sit up and laugh. Then I approached the last minute of the speech, the bit that clever people will sometimes call the 'peroration'. This is the moment when the speaker sums up the argument and inspires the audience.

For some reason I saw the end coming and started to panic a little bit.

"Don't worry, I'm nearly finished," I said. "The rant is nearly over." Cue puzzled looks in the audience. It wasn't a rant. They had been enjoying it. But for some reason I'd felt the need to say that.

As it happens, I still won the competition. At the end, however, one of the old fellows took me to one side. "Great speech, but *never apologise*," he said.

One lesson for me from that day was: yes, do everything you can to make your speech or presentation as interesting and engaging as possible. But when you are up on that stage, it is *your* moment. You are not an interlude before something more interesting comes along. You are the main attraction. If you think it, you can become it.

Another lesson was: *enjoy* the climax. Don't build to the big moment then pull back through lack of confidence. Go for it.

After the beginning, the ending of the speech is the most important part. If you get it right, the last words you say should ring in the ears of the audience and echo in their memories. Think back to recent business speeches you have heard – can you remember the ending? Or did the speaker make his or her points and then just fizzle out and waffle over the finish line?

Even if you are improvising much of the talk, you need to have the ending absolutely nailed, and probably memorised. If you don't, it's a missed opportunity. Knowing the ending will also give you the confidence to relax and go off-script in the middle section, because you can always come back confidently on-script for the finale.

Approaching the ending, that's the moment you need to change gear. Either you will up the tempo to your crescendo, or slow things... right down... so the words... at the close... carry the maximum... weight and... impact.

Avoid the familiar trap of the false ending(s): "And by way of conclusion... and if there's one more thing I'd like to say... and just before I sit down... and just before I wrap up, because I'm conscious of time... so finally, four points I'd like to share..." Ahhhhhh!

The ending must be the ending. It must feel like the ending. The audience must feel confident that the speaker knows the final destination. Then they will happily let you be their guide.

Some of the most famous perorations in history had a highly charged and emotional call to action. One of the best was Winston Churchill's 'finest hour' speech. The ending was so strong that the last two words – 'finest hour' – provided the title for the speech.

Churchillian rhetoric probably won't be appropriate for your annual results day or the opening of a new branch office, but you can get away with being more emotionally charged than normal as you wrap things up.

Here are a few end options to consider:

Loop back
If you've made a bold statement at the beginning (see previous section), loop back to it at the end:

- "And that is how we meet that ambition to be the best in the world at IT. Thank you very much".
- "And if we do all of these things, and work together as a team, we will achieve our target of doubling sales. Thank you very much".

Answer the question

If you posed a big question at the beginning of the speech, the ending can be the moment to provide the definitive answer:

- "So, coming back to the question I asked at the beginning: how do we provide both high return and security of income? We do it by investing. Investing in technology and investing in people. Thank you very much".

Call to action

Your speech up until this point has been convincing the audience of the argument, so the ending is: OK, what should we do about it?

- "I want everyone in this room to go back to their offices. Over the next few days, I want each of you to choose one of your clients, look back at their file and see what problems they were grappling with last month. Pick up the phone and call them. Don't try to sell them something. Just see how they got on with the issue. Then next month, we'll share what we've learnt from those conversations. Thank you very much".

Cast forward

You might consider ending your speech by casting forward into the future, providing hope or inspiration about what is to come:

- "So when we meet in a year's time, what will we have achieved? I hope three things: X, Y and Z. I look forward to that moment when we can say: yes, we did it. Thank you very much".

Story

I'm including this one somewhat reluctantly. Some good speeches are ruined by the words "Before I finish I'd like to tell you a story". *Here we go*, the audience is thinking. *We're stuck here for another five minutes.* However, a story or anecdote might be an effective way to finish, particularly if there is a memorable punchline that sums up the theme in some way. But be careful. I think you need to tell your end story in a minute or less, or you risk undoing your earlier work.

However you choose to end, it's important to signal that *it is the end*. Deliver your last point, bow your head slightly and close. Then don't rush from the stage like a frightened animal. Hold your position for a few seconds, maintaining eye contact with the audience.

Thank you very much.

Pitch It

Pitching can be the most daunting – and exciting – part of business. Getting a small team together and going into a room for an hour in front of a stern-looking panel is enough to induce a knee tremor in the most battle-hardened pro.

Successful pitches, however, are the champagne moments. They are the ones you look back on and remember with a little glow.

Those in PR agencies are forever pitching to potential new clients. The pitch is the classic business set piece – a condensed sell, with real money on the line, and (often) a genuinely uncertain outcome.

In one of the pitches I was involved with, we had prepared hard for three to four weeks and explored every angle of the client's problem, with exhaustive research and interviews. The fruit of our labour was a beautiful booklet, setting out a clear and effective communications strategy, with a detailed action plan.

On the big day, the CEO stormed into the room.

"I don't want to talk about anything you've prepared. Put the document away," he snapped.

Instead he set us a completely new, and very odd, challenge, which we spent the next hour brainstorming. We had to think on our feet as never before. It was bizarre. It was uncomfortable. We won the business. But it was never a happy client relationship.

Normally, the team does get to present its ideas. Here, often, the enemy is boredom. The client/investor/customer might be seeing 5–10 different teams, all trotting out the same platitudes and 'insights'.

A lot of pitches are like an unfunny episode of *The Apprentice*. A team of misfits throws together a set of slides telling the host obvious things. This 'presentation' is then delivered in a rather manic, jittery, but incredibly bland style.

In their book *Life's a Pitch*, Roger Mavity and co-author Stephen Bayley deconstruct the pitch, which they define very broadly to include all the significant moments that can lead to crucial shifts. They could be formal business pitches or more personal moments, like asking someone out or persuading the bank to give you a loan.

The pitch, says Mavity, is the 'hinge' for the door in life's most important moments. Every pitch, every presentation, is a balance between excitement and reassurance. You want to get people to sit up, take notice, see the possibilities... but not to scare them. You also want to be solid, dependable, employable, safe.

This is as much about how you make people *feel* as what you tell them.

Mavity argues that, because you're asking someone to make a call on the future – and they can't – their judgement won't be based on logical factors but on emotional signals: trust, confidence, desire. They are instinctive. You can't process them. But you base your decision on them nevertheless.

It's often said that 'people buy people'. The team in the room is more important than the ideas on the page or the screen. This is true. You do, however, need to have something decent prepared, with a clear story and at least one memorable thought.

"My philosophy," said Nick Barron, deputy CEO of the communications agency MHP, on the *PR for Humans* podcast, "is to try to say something interesting as quickly as possible. Show them that we've been doing some thinking. Here's what the problem is. Here's our take."

The best pitches, it is sometimes said, are the ones you never have to do – the client/investor/customer simply decides they want you. This does, though, remove some of the drama and excitement.

In competitive situations with lots of suitors, the marriage offer could go to anyone because there are so many imponderables, from the time of day, to the temperature in the room, to the quality of the biscuits on the table. At that point, assuming there are no obvious and glaring flaws with any of the line-up, it's very hard to say who will land the proposal.

So, relax. Try to be interesting. Make it more of a conversation and less of a presentation. Ask the host questions. Get some interaction going. And don't be silly.

Nick Barron advises extreme caution with the themed pitch:

> When I was at the Football Association, every agency that came to see us would say 'this is a pitch of two halves' or they would introduce themselves dressed in their football kit or whatever. Unbearable. I've seen every permutation of the football-themed pitch that you ever want to see.

If you force a theme into your pitch, you'll lose subtlety and the essential quality of *the conversation*.

Know Your Audience

In 1995, our undergraduate theatre group took a production of *Hamlet* to South Korea... by mistake.

A Seoul-based media company was looking for a top English drama troupe to bring Shakespeare on tour and perform in a 2,000-seat venue in the South Korean capital. Initially they approached the Royal Shakespeare Company (RSC). Having been rebuffed, they looked for an alternative and stumbled upon the Amateur Dramatic Club (ADC) in Cambridge, which boasted luminaries such as Sir Ian McKellen, Emma Thompson, Peter Hall and Sam Mendes among its former members.

RSC? ADC? They must have looked very similar from a South Korean perspective in the mid-90s. But of course, the ADC was run by students and the word 'amateur' was in the title for a reason. There were some talented people in our group, like Simon Kane, Gus Brown, Ed Waters and Simon Godwin (who interestingly did go on to direct *Hamlet* at the RSC). But at that time, we were a bunch of 18-, 19- and 20-year-old undergraduates messing around. When the fax came through offering us not just flights and five-star accommodation but a performance fee of £20,000, we thought it was a bizarre hoax.

We carried on rehearsing our version of *Hamlet* (minimalist, modern dress) for the upcoming performances. The annual ADC tour of student campuses in the USA had long been arranged. We had our work cut out to prepare for that and we didn't think much more of the South Korean invitation. Then, one day, a man called Mr Kim arrived and sat quietly in the back of the Cambridge rehearsal room. Mr Kim didn't appear to speak any English, but we smiled at him and shook his hand a lot. Goodness knows what he thought of our show. He must have provided a vaguely positive report, though, because the plane tickets and the money came through. We would fly from London to New York to Seoul and take *Hamlet* around the world. I had the plum part of the evil Claudius.

The audiences in the USA and South Korea were *very* different. They would be much closer now, I suspect, in culture and expectations. But back in 1995 it really *felt* like they were on opposite sides of the world. The college campuses we played on in Washington DC, Baltimore and Philadelphia were cool and modern. They loved our subtle, English, understated *Hamlet* – acted like a movie. But in South Korea we were given a stern pep talk after the dress rehearsal.

"More emotion! More action!" shouted Mr Kim's boss.

We had already swapped our modern dress for traditional Shakespearian garb. Now they wanted us to adopt hammed-up Korean acting techniques too. And, as I quickly learnt, the client is always right. We pumped up the passion and gesticulated with gusto. "Good!" shouted Mr Kim's boss. Mr Kim himself stayed silent.

Then it was show time. Complete unknowns in any country, we were mobbed for autographs outside the barn-like theatre in downtown Seoul. Two thousand people packed in to see our *Hamlet*. And the reaction? Let's just say the critics were divided.

Half the audience walked out during the show. That's right, 1,000 people walked out during every performance. I will never forget being on stage and seeing the rows of seats emptying as we struggled to hold our audience, to literally keep them in place. But those who stayed *loved* it. We received wild standing ovations from the remaining 1,000 at the end of each show.

When I think about audiences, I think back to the strange and wonderful South Korea tour all those years ago. If there is a lesson, it is this: you've got to deliver something that matches the expectations of your audience. Whether it's a play or a speech or a video or a media interview, the audience really is everything – their opinions, their knowledge, their cultural references. The better you understand the audience, the more effective you will be as a communicator.

This brings us from Shakespeare all the way back to Aristotle. In Aristotle's communication model, the role of the speaker is to convince an audience. But he also believed that different messages and different speeches should be made for different audiences. Aristotle said that you have to prepare a speech with the target audience in mind. You've got to understand who they are, the things they care about and the expectations they have. If you don't have knowledge of your audience, you have very little chance of reaching them or moving them.

You don't need to love the audience. But you do need to try to understand them. A speech flops when the speaker doesn't take the time to get to know their audience. It crashes when the speaker doesn't care about the audience and doesn't in any way seek to make them feel involved or special. Seriously misjudge the spectators and you get communications calamity.

Know your audience. Flatter them. Involve them. Play to them. Win them. Keep them.

These are the rules when you own the stage. But what about when you are not speaking but chairing? The principles of clarity, energy, humility and the rest still apply, with a few little twists.

Be a Proper Chair

As the person chairing an event, you can be the trusted figure of authority without having to stick your neck out with any opinions. It's less arduous to prepare for than if you're delivering the keynote. And yet, so many panel discussions are badly chaired. So many leadership opportunities are missed.

As the chair, you should be the host but not the star. The main thing to remember is that *you are on the side of the audience*. Humility. This is where so many people go wrong. They think they are on the side of the panellists. Or they think they are the main speaker. The introductions are indulgent, the contributors ramble on, the audience doesn't get the opportunity to be involved or shape the discussion.

The chair must be the audience's representative on the stage, always asking themselves: is this what the audience came for? Are they getting something interesting? Is the discussion moving along? Is one person hogging the debate? Is there overall clarity?

BBC radio producers won't book guests who agree with each other on everything. You need a bit of tension and a bit of debate. Not hostile argument, but a little bit of crackle. It's the same with a panel discussion. As the moderator, you need to ensure that the differences and shades of opinion are clear to the audience.

Find your own personal style. From charming host, to urgent inquisitor, to fiery examiner, to funny self-deprecator, to heavyweight challenger – there are lots of options. The one thing all good chairs will do, though, is seek a balance of views and ensure the audience gets to hear them.

You've got to keep the discussion moving forward. You need to keep things relevant for the audience. And, perhaps most importantly, you need to finish on time (or ideally a few minutes early). I've never heard anyone complain when the bell rings slightly early. If, as chair, you let things overrun, you've failed, in my view. Failed in your main responsibility: to get the audience out on time, feeling that they've heard something interesting.

This is all a lot easier if, at the planning stage, you've worked with your team to come up with a clear topic for the event. Many panels suffer from not having a properly defined theme. Are you assembling the guests to answer a big question? Is there one key idea that you'd like to explore? As chair you need to know what the story is. Ideally, you will gather the panellists in advance (or get a conference call together) to talk it through.

As with writing an article or a speech, you may want to write a headline for the event, even if it's a headline with a question mark. The topic should be one on which there is a genuine difference of views.

It can't be something like 'Why investment underpins business success'. That's too bland to be a good theme for a panel discussion. Nobody could really disagree with that statement. There's no tension, and no proper debate.

There must be at least two sides to the argument. Your job as chair is then to be the central pivot of the debate. Inevitably, things will veer off in different directions. People will say unexpected things. Some audience interventions can be a bit left field. As chair, you've got to restore balance.

One exercise I do with clients wanting to improve their moderating skills is to set up a 'speed chairing' game. Here's how it works:

Assemble five people and sit them down as if on the platform at a conference. Each one gets to play the chair – and sit in the central seat – for five minutes. When they are not the chair, they are the panellists. There's a bell which I ring each time the chair does something good. The players get:

- A point for introducing each panellist quickly and clearly
- A point for picking up on something one panellist has said and putting it to someone else
- A point for a witty intervention
- A point for involving the audience
- A point for thanking each panellist quickly and clearly
- Two points for finishing within five minutes!

This exercise is a lot of fun and has resulted in some rather ponderous characters suddenly becoming super-energised MCs. Give it a go with your leadership team.

Own the Panel

Being *on the panel* is a very different assignment from the role of chair. The first questions you should be asking yourself are: why have I been chosen in this line-up? How does the organiser think my perspective will be different from the other people on the stage?

Panellists should be chosen for one of two reasons: either their knowledge complements that of the other members, or they are likely to give a different opinion on the key issue being discussed. Lots of panels fail because there's no clarity or logic to the assembly. The views and perspectives on the platform are too similar. There isn't a big question that they can all provide a different take on. Often (rightly) the panel needs to be diverse – in terms of gender and in other ways. This can make the argument even harder to define.

On the day, this isn't your problem. You just need to be the best version of yourself.

If you are chosen for a panel, the first thing you need to do is have a mini keynote prepared. Even if you're not asked to give a set speech, you need to have about five minutes of material organised as you would for any short talk. You must have a clear headline for the event. You need a topical reference ready. You might have thought of a story/anecdote that connects you to the question of the day. Ideally you will describe a visual example or case study that brings it to life. You might even have a great metaphor that you've developed to carry the idea. You will know what your call to action is for those in the audience.

This material might be (mostly) delivered as an answer to the opening question, which is usually quite general. Or you could sprinkle it across a few different answers. A judgement can be made on the day.

Make no mistake, a panel is a competition. The audience will be ranking the contributors. In the coffee break afterwards, they will be talking about their favourite. Of course, you want to win the panel. But winning will require a lot of listening and a lot of humility.

If you go on the panel and try to steamroller the other guests out of the conversation, the audience will write you off. If you're always trying to edge into every moment, you'll annoy everyone in the hall. A business panel isn't a TV comedy show. Here, first prize goes to the person who can:

- Express their own perspective with superb clarity and concision
- Find memorable language or at least one good story/visual example
- Listen carefully to the other guests, compliment them and respond to them
- Make a real effort to understand the audience's questions, and answer only the ones they are best qualified to tackle
- Come across as calm, relaxed, moderate and humble

In a panel, smile.

Smile when you're being introduced. Listen attentively. Smile and nod when another panellist makes a good point. Laugh easily, but not too noisily. Smile at the end. Don't rush off the stage. Stay chatting after the final whistle.

One other tip: a chair will often ask each guest for one big thought at the end (a prediction for the year ahead, their best memory of the election, a phrase that sums up their advice – whatever). These things are hard to think up in the heat of the moment. If you're chatting casually with the chair before the show, ask them whether the panellists will be asked for a summary thought at the end, and what that might be. You can then prepare your 'spontaneous' witty remark.

In panels, you've got to be the nicest, most seemingly generous person on the stage. Humility! But you also need to be the person with ideas and comments so sharp they might have been cut by a laser.

This is only possible with preparation. Just because it's a panel rather than a set-piece speech doesn't mean you can just rock up on the day and hope for the best.

Preparation is the best way to improve PERFORMANCE, the subject of the next chapter.

Summary

- **Make it personal:** It's your moment and you need to start your preparation by looking inwards and back at your own story. Which moments might you highlight to bring out a theme?

- **Have a clear idea:** Great speeches have a single big idea. This is sometimes called the 'topic'. A proper topic needs an argument. The case you're making in the speech has got to be arguable. Someone out there must be able to disagree with what you're saying.

- **Work hard on the beginning and end:** The bit in the middle doesn't matter quite as much. Audiences focus on the beginning and the end. If you start and finish strong, you will be remembered for that. You might start with a story, a joke or a question. At the end, try to loop back to the thought at the beginning.

- **Flatter the audience:** A speech is more about the audience than you. *PR for Humans* is always about the audience. Think carefully about them beforehand. Design the speech for them. Flatter them. Play to the gallery.

- **When chairing, be on the side of the audience:** As chair, you're not on the side of your chums on the panel; you're the *audience's* representative on stage. You've got to keep the discussion moving. Make it interesting and relevant. If you're on the panel, prepare as if for a speech.

2. PERFORMANCE

*The best way to improve your performance is to run a checklist against the principles of
PR for Humans.*

Belief. Clarity. Opinion. Energy. Context. Time. Humility. Imagery.

*Get those right and you won't need to worry too much about the technical aspects of
speech delivery. If the material is clear, if you believe in it, if you show the right energy,
give your backstory, stake out a position, use visual language and don't seem too
arrogant – well, you're 90% there!*

*But, specifically, what do else to we need to know to carry the audience? This chapter
takes you through the art of performance, starting with body language.*

Clench

It is sometimes said that effective communication is 10% what you say and
90% how you say it. Over time, various pseudo-scientific studies have been
done to support this notion. I'm not sure I totally agree with it, but there's
no doubting the importance of delivery.

You can take the very same speech, give it to two different people to
perform and the outcome will be vastly different. How we use our voices and
our bodies matters hugely. Few people in business invest any time, however,
in developing their physical performance skills.

Some speakers pace up and down the stage, making their audiences feel
rather seasick. Some flap their hands around, looking out of control. Some
refuse ever to emerge from behind the lectern, gripping onto it for dear life.
Some stand rigidly in one spot, with their hands behind their backs, in their
pockets or rigidly down at their sides.

Some act at being the great 'thought leader', moving around, pausing and
emoting, despite the rather empty content of the actual speech. Comedian
Pat Kelly has done a brilliant satirical take-off of the absurd delivery style of
some faux TED talks with his (completely substance-free) speech about what
it means to be a 'thought leader'. Look it up on YouTube. It's hilarious. He
gives a commentary on everything he's doing on stage as he's doing it:

> You can tell I'm a thought leader because I've just done this [holds
> fingers together] with my hands... now if it's OK I'm going to pace
> while telling you this story... walking over here I'm going to change the
> tone of my voice and tell you something completely unrelated.[29]

It's a particularly good sketch. The speech is about absolutely nothing,
but it's delivered as if every word matters. And it's riveting.

Body language, though, is easy to mock. Anyone can look or sound
silly very easily on stage. Here are a few simple guidelines for avoiding those
mistakes:

There are occasions when a rigid and very straight delivery style is
needed. If you are announcing a big redundancy programme, or the results
of a public inquiry, then forget about pacing around. Go to the lectern and
read it out. This shows the gravity of the situation. Sometimes the material
could be legally sensitive and the speech should be delivered word for word.
If the speech is going to be published then this sort of address is really a
'spoken essay'. These can be moments of great authority for a leader, so don't
discount them.

In general, though, the podium will be a barrier to the audience. Try, if
you can, to step out from behind it and come towards the audience – take
centre stage. You should be aiming for a solid stance, with equal balance on
each leg, shoulders down, head up (but not too far up – your chin mustn't
be up in the air).

At first, hold your hands together loosely in front of your stomach.
This is an open gesture and allows you to feel secure without putting up a
defensive barrier to your audience. You can also hold speaking notes or cue
cards in this position. Occasionally, make simple, confident and clear hand
gestures during the talk. You may even walk a few paces on the stage. But
then find your balanced position again, with your hands loosely held in the
same position.

On body language, and other aspects of delivery, I learnt a lot from actor
and communication coach Robin Kermode, author of the excellent guide
Speak So Your Audience Will Listen. Speaking on my podcast, he told me the
best body language tip I've ever heard for developing extra charisma. It's all
about the buttocks:

> If you walk to the centre of the stage, you then clench the buttock
> muscles or the thigh muscles... you lock those two big muscle groups –

---

[29] Pat Kelly, thought leader speech: www.youtube.com/watch?v=_ZBKX-6Gz6A

one or both – the buttocks and the thighs. This will lower your centre of gravity. You tend not to move around so much. It's impossible to shake. Your voice gets more centred and you look more centred. It's a very simple technique.

So, go ahead – clench your buttocks and feel like a leader.

(Try Not To) Use Slides

Former colleagues may find it amusing that I am writing advice on using PowerPoint. During my 18 years in journalism, I didn't produce a single slide or present any decks at all.

In fact, I first heard the term 'deck' in 2014 and didn't know what it meant. For those still in the dark, it's a set of PowerPoint slides.

In my first couple of years in business, I felt horribly exposed whenever slides were required for a pitch or a meeting. Looking back, I should have been far more confident about my skills and experience as a news presenter. I should have stuck most of these 'presentations' where they belonged – in the real or virtual recycle bin.

The fact is that most people in PR and communications don't know how to use visual aids to get their message across. Too often slides are the enemy of *PR for Humans*. But it's not the technology that's to blame; it's the way that it's used.

Here's a summary of some of the questions you could be asking yourself ahead of a presentation:

Do I need slides at all?
Sometimes slides are produced simply because there is a presentation coming up, and the feeling is that a deck will be needed to show that the proper amount of work has been done. This is a mistake. If you can talk without slides, go for it. Alternatives might include: drawing on a white board, playing a video, using props, handing out pictures or (try this!) simply talking directly to the people in the room.

How many slides do I need?
There's a common misconception that the problem with a bad deck is often the number of slides. No, the far bigger problem is the content and the clutter: overloaded and badly thought through slides. Most presentations try to convey too much information, but the number of slides you use depends entirely on what's on them.

From my days as a TV news reporter, I know that a five-minute television report may contain as many as 70–80 different shots (more if there's a high-speed montage). We can happily absorb this as audiences because the human brain is very good at processing images. So if your slides are basically just images, a presentation with 20–30 slides could be OK. But if those slides are covered in bullet points and graphs and numbers and long titles and subtitles, 20–30 slides will probably kill most people in the audience.

So many people get it the wrong way around. They work on the slides first, as if the slides are the presentation. No, the presentation is you. The slides are just there to make you look better. First, work out the argument that you are trying to pitch. Find the golden thread that runs through it all. Clarity! Map out the stages and transitions that you'll need to make. Then – and only once you have a good idea of what it's all about – create the slides.

Should I make two versions of the deck?

Ninety per cent of problems with slides arise because people are essentially trying to present slides that are designed to be sent over email and read. These text-heavy decks should never be presented. The audience will either read ahead and spend the whole presentation looking at the screen rather than at you, or they will just switch off altogether.

So make two versions. The one you present can be mainly images and, perhaps, a big number (in bold) on a couple of slides. The one you email out afterwards can have all the information the audience will need to reference later.

Can I shake things up?

Look at the way Google's CEO, Sundar Pichai, does his presentations at Google I/O, the company's annual developer conference. He uses slides, but they are all simple and all different. Slide 1 might be a series of logos. Slide 2, a clear graph showing subscriber growth. Slide 3, a huge photo montage. Slide 4, a dancing robot. And so on. Every slide is beautifully simple, but every slide uses a different format, keeping the audience engaged.

Can I just put up one slide?

Maybe you could be bold and focus on a single slide that really encapsulates the problem you're here to solve. I've seen this done at conferences quite effectively, with the line "I don't want to bore you with lots of slides, so I've brought just one – here it is". But even this one slide must be simple and uncluttered.

Visual storytelling is, as we've already discussed, so important for anyone wanting to attempt *PR for Humans*. It's sad that the most powerful visual presenting tools are misused every single day, in thousands upon thousands of offices and at hundreds of conferences and events.

So go at your decks: cut slides, make them more visual, cut information and shake things up. Work out the clear and believable story you want to tell *before* you even open PowerPoint.

Sometimes I have slides prepared but I don't get around to presenting them in the room because the conversation has already become more interesting and interactive than the slides could ever be. Those are the good days.

Use Props (Sometimes)

At primary school, my sons were often asked to do a 'show-and-tell'. They would take in an object (preferably not a toy), stand up in front of their class and talk about it. In doing this, the children were linking an idea or a set of memories to something physical.

I was often surprised that the boys really wanted to do show-and-tells and even looked forward to them. They never saw it as 'public speaking'. They never seemed nervous or shy about it. And, like all children, they absolutely loved telling people about things they were proud of.

Show-and-tell is a way for children to practise both talking to an audience and being part of an audience: speaking and listening to others. In many schools, this is now seen as an important part of the education process. The little people doing show-and-tells are learning how to be storytellers and how to use props.

I don't remember ever doing this at school. Although we did a lot of drama, I didn't stand up in front of the class and present anything. The focus was all on the 'three Rs' and keeping your head down.[30]

Many business executives of a certain age are in the same boat. We weren't taught in school how to present, so we've had to learn it when it's much harder – as adults. We can still, though, take inspiration from the show-and-tell approach.

Many dull speeches are brought to life by props.

---

[30] The three Rs are commonly reading, writing and arithmetic.

One famous example is a 2008 TED talk given by Jill Bolte Taylor, a brain scientist who suffered a massive stroke and watched her own brain functions shut down one by one. To illustrate this, Taylor brought a *real human brain* onto the stage and held it up before the audience.[31]

Despite the powerful emotional story, this talk by a neuroscientist might well have been forgotten, but holding the real brain on stage made it unforgettable. People are still talking about the talk more than a decade later.

You don't have to be as extreme as that in your selection and use of props. But what should you choose?

Anyone in a consumer product industry has it easy in this regard: you can simply pass around your most intriguing item (if it is small enough). I attended a nice talk at Boodles jewellery store, where the owner passed around a huge diamond and then asked everyone to guess its value.

Those working in financial or professional services might have to work harder for their impact, but props can still be used to make your personal story a little more concrete. Here are some examples:

- If, as an international property mogul, you want to talk about your struggle to save for a deposit on your first home, you could hold up the key to that home, or show a photo of the day you moved in.
- If you came to New York for the first time 20 years ago to launch your banking career, you could bring along the battered old city guidebook you still have.
- If a client ever gave you a little gift or memento, you could carry it with you to illustrate the importance of client service.

Real items can make a talk more interesting, more real. They can give extra definition to your character. They can illustrate your backstory and show where you've come from.

As well as the specific items for your set piece, many of the great leaders in history had their signature items and props that they would carry or wear everywhere. Lincoln had his hat. Churchill had his cigars and black-rimmed glasses. Thatcher had her handbags.

The props became extensions of the characters of these leaders. They helped to create and maintain the aura. One minister even remembered a day when Margaret Thatcher couldn't attend a Cabinet meeting. Instead,

---

[31] Jill Bolte Taylor, TED talk: www.ted.com/talks/jill_bolte_taylor_s_powerful_stroke_of_insight

she left her huge handbag in the middle of the table. The bag still dominated the meeting. Or so the story goes.

Find Your Voice

So much of the energy and emotion of your performance comes from your voice rather than your body language, although the two are of course connected. A strong, resonant voice will help you to communicate with more power and impact.

As with so much in communication, a lot is down to genetics. But you can certainly work to develop a deeper, more impactful voice that people will pay attention to.

Actors spend years at drama school honing and training their voices, allowing them to fill large auditoriums with mellifluous tones. Business leaders don't have time to spend years learning breathing techniques and finding their deeper selves. These days, any event of any size will have microphones that can amplify even the weediest voices to fill the chamber. That means that many in business don't think voice matters as much. Big mistake.

Later in the book (Part 2, Chapter 5), we will discuss the power of audio (in radio and podcasting), and it's my belief that the human voice remains one of the most important tools in the armoury of anyone wanting to practise *PR for Humans*.

So many 'meetings' and 'presentations' in business now take place on conference calls. Sometimes there is a video link, sometimes not. It's often the case that your voice is the only thing that connects you to the audience. You need to be able to command the room (or conference call) with the sound of your words.

Lisa Åkesson is a voice coach with more than 20 years of experience with RADA (the Royal Academy of Dramatic Art) and she works with business leaders all over the world. On the *PR for Humans* podcast, she told me that voices need to be trained to create the right impact. For men, the depth – that sound of authority – can come more easily than for women. But, male or female, all speakers benefit from finding deeper resonance:

> Your lungs need to breathe deeply. The movement of the diaphragm is downwards. You are creating a cavern in your chest. The voice bounces off the bone structure in the ribcage. That gives chest resonance. That's the gravitas sound. But if I just stay down there, it can be dull.

So, to inspire, we need to move upwards, with more brightness and energy, higher in the range.

For me, this is the critical point: depth is good, but variety is essential. The worst is monotone – an utter disconnect between thoughts, emotions and sound.

The way you use your voice must reflect the things going on in your mind. A smiley voice *sounds smiley*. A frowny voice *sounds frowny*. A doubtful voice *sounds doubtful*. The emotion, the physical expression and the voice are all linked. If we read or present without having the correct emotions and thoughts in our heads, we will sound robotic.

If, however, we want to connect with a real human audience, we have to find the variety and shifts of tone to match the transitions and opinions in our story.

One way of doing this is to mark the key moments very clearly on your text. Smile here. Now slow down. Pause. Increase pace. Breathe. Now brightness! Inspiration! Coming to the serious bit. Slow. Lower tone. Breathe.

Don't go overboard with 'voice coaching'. It's hard to get results and so easy to sound like a fake. Better to use your voice deliberately to show the audience what you really think and believe. The secret of 'authenticity' is in the performance.

Dress the Best

Very few people will have selected this book for its advice on style and fashion, but there's no doubt that the clothes you wear are a big part of the story you're telling, whether you like it or not. To play the part, you must look the part. That doesn't mean dazzling audiences with the latest items off the catwalks of London or Milan. It does mean taking a step back and having an awareness of the image you are projecting.

When I was a reporter on Sky News, the editor stopped me in the corridor one day and told me, in no uncertain terms, that I was a mess. I needed a haircut. I needed better clothes. At the time I was embarrassed and offended, and pretty much ignored the advice. But looking back now, I think I should have been more self-aware. If I wanted to be a top correspondent, I had to look like a top correspondent. It sounds so obvious. Image matters.

The whole issue of what to wear professionally is possibly a simpler one for men than for women. Men can usually create a strong enough impression with good suits, nice shirts and well-made shoes. You won't set the world on fire, but nor will you lose a deal or a promotion because you don't look like a leader.

For women, the waters of style are more treacherous. Lizzie Edwards is a fashion consultant and adviser to senior professionals. On the *PR for Humans* podcast, she told me that the core of the issue for women is that clothes are so important, but they can also so easily take the focus away from the things you're saying and the person you need to be:

> When people get to a certain level, they don't want to look the same as everyone else, but equally they don't want to be distracting. The worst thing is if the audience is not listening to what you're saying because they are distracted by what you are wearing.

It's hard to lay down any rules in this area, because every situation (pitch, presentation, conference speech, TV interview) will be different. On each occasion, we are seeking to project the right balance of excitement and reassurance. But Lizzie's advice is simply to *stop* and *think carefully* about the person *you are* and the person *you want to be*, on a given day.

As the audience, we make judgements about the speaker and the story based partly on the clothes they wear. A certain way of dressing can also change how *you* feel, make you more confident and decisive or nervy and scruffy. In the world of humans, it all matters.

Your uniform needs to be credible, though. You must believe in the role. The clothes must give you the right positive energy.

I'll save the rest of my fashion advice for another book. But, I emphasise again – this stuff *is* important. Even if clothes bore you, they will interest at least half of the people in the audience.

PR for Humans is about the real person you are inside. But it's also about how you project and perform. You need the right outfit to play each part, so when preparing for a speech, a pitch or an interview, ask: how do I want to be seen?

As well as working on the script, spend some time thinking about the costume you need to wear – for that audience, at that moment.

Memorise (Occasionally)

A question I often get asked is: should I try to memorise my speech?

It's certainly possible. The human brain is capable of amazing feats of memory. Many Muslim children memorise the entire Koran. The best memory champions in the world can learn the order of a newly shuffled deck of cards in about 20 seconds. Lead actors can go on stage and deliver a complex sequence of words and movements in precisely the same order for over two hours a night.

How do they do it?

Developing the memory – or at least mastering some memory tricks – can make a leader seem much more impressive. Anyone who can stand up confidently and recall names, places, ideas, stories and arguments will be regarded as a very strong and powerful communicator.

If you want to memorise a speech or presentation, there are two main options: memorise word for word, or memorise a sequence of ideas and images.

The first is harder and takes more time. This is essentially what I used to do as a student actor. You read your lines aloud again and again, with the text in front of you at first, and then you gradually start covering up portions of text and trying to recall the lines. This usually needs to happen over a period of days to be effective. It's particularly useful to read over the lines last thing at night; during sleep they can solidify into memory. You must be very focused and clear your mind of other distractions. It helps to 'act out' the lines a bit, to put them into the context of a scene, so each line corresponds with a position on the stage or an interaction with someone.

With 'by rote' memorisation, there's a difference between knowing it and *knowing it*. My rule is that only when you can recite the lines out loud at two or three times normal speaking speed, either recorded or in front of someone, at least twice do you *know it*. Then you need to keep the mental imprint of the words fresh by revisiting it several times a day at first, then at least every couple of weeks afterwards. If the imprint is deep enough, you can recall speeches and poems that you first learnt decades earlier. Often, the key is the rhythm of the language. Verse is easier to remember than prose. Just as we have amazing recall and memory of music, so can we remember words that form patterns.

This brings us on to the second main technique: memorising sequences. This can give you the ability to stand up and deliver a long speech without notes or cue cards.

The human brain loves patterns. It also loves visual cues. But those people with the best memories are the ones who know how to use their hippocampus. This is the part of the brain responsible for navigation and spatial awareness. Unless this part of the brain has been damaged, every human being can navigate through complex, three-dimensional space.

Think of your journey to work, a route you regularly drive or walk, or your knowledge of how to move around a familiar large building or campus. You can learn what seem like very complex sequences by ascribing an idea or an image to each part of a walk or place that you already know well. This method is called the Memory Palace. It's said to have been thought up 2,500 years ago by the Ancient Greek poet Simonides. He was attending a banquet in Thessalia. While he was outside, the hall's ceiling collapsed, killing everyone. The corpses were mangled and unrecognisable. But Simonides could easily remember who was sitting where, because he knew the layout of the palace so well. If you can remember – in physical space – the layout of a building or a seating plan by visualising it, you can also ascribe abstract memories to specific locations.

Through the ages (including, notably, Cicero in Roman times), orators were able to remember long speeches by thinking of the talk as a walk around their house or a palace they knew well. Each idea – or, in the modern context, 'bullet point' – is given an image that is then placed in a certain part of that building.

So, if the first thing you need to do in a speech is thank the team and celebrate the year's achievements, *imagine a big colourful 'Congratulations' balloon attached to your front door.*

If the next thing you want to do is tell a little anecdote about Halloween, *imagine a giant pumpkin in your hallway.*

If you then want to talk about customer growth, *imagine a huge, inflatable, grinning customer expanding to fill your kitchen.*

If you then want to warn about the dangers of overexpansion, *imagine that inflatable customer catching fire on the hob and blowing up in flames.*

If you then want to talk about the wider market challenges, *imagine a market trader has set up a stall selling cheese in your living room.*

In your mind's eye, walk around your house (or palace, if you have one) and see the sequence of ideas that you need to follow. The more absurd and ridiculous the images are, the easier they will be to remember. This is far, far easier and more reliable than trying to remember a list of bullet points or numbers on a piece of paper.

The work thinking up the silly images to go with each room in the house takes a little bit of time. Once you've done that, however, the memorisation is a piece of cake – which you can munch on your way out of your Memory Palace.

I've used this technique myself several times and taught it to clients. It works best when you have a very clear idea what the 7–10 things are that you want to say in your speech and the order that you want to say them in. If you have two or three speeches coming up, you can't use your own house more than once! Instead, you might use your route to work or to the gym. You must use real locations, though. Imagining a fictitious Memory Palace is less effective and unnecessary.

Memorising isn't for everyone. For some people, it will always be too risky. If you lose their thread midway through, it can bring calamity.

But for those with the time to prepare properly, and the knowledge of some simple tricks, it can result in very powerful performances. Just be sure that when you get up there, you don't just know it, you *really know it*.

Rehearse Seriously

The best rehearsals are the ones closest to the performance. Think of a dress rehearsal the day before the opening night of a show. You're wearing the costume, the make-up has been applied, the house lights go down, all the props and visual effects are ready – then you go and practise the show *exactly as you will perform the real thing*.

The 'rehearsals' most business leaders have ahead of their set-piece moments are miles away from the real thing. Picture the scene: the CEO huddled in a stuffy meeting room with the communications chief, the marketing head, maybe someone from a PR agency. They're going through slides, discussing the bullet points on each one. They're reading out sections of a pre-written text, scribbling notes. People are scurrying around checking facts and figures. A new picture is needed for slide 17. The title of the speech needs changing. Have we got the date wrong on slide 7? Quick, fire off an email to someone in the strategy team. The CEO finally gets to have a run-through in the last 15 minutes of allotted time. Then the poor advisers gabble a few feedback points as the boss rushes off to the next meeting.

That's not a rehearsal. That's a mess. I know, I've been in that room, and the actual speech was even more shambolic.

A rehearsal should be just that: a rehearsal. OK, don't worry about the make-up and the costume, but everything else should be signed and sealed. If possible, you will be in the location that you will be in to deliver the real speech. If not, get the biggest room you can find. Invite a few people. The closer you can make it to the real thing, the more effective it will be. Because, make no mistake, rehearsal is vital. Absolutely critical. The best business presenters take their cue from Steve Jobs. They practise... obsessively.

A good rehearsal – just like a proper dress rehearsal for actors – is only possible if a heck of a lot of work has been done in the days and weeks ahead: writing scripts, honing the story, cutting lines, cutting scenes. Preparation that is often done the day before should be happening a couple of weeks before. This will give the star the time they need to learn their lines and feel comfortable in character.

Once you have your building blocks well cemented, the actual rehearsal can proceed smoothly. You might start with a 'walk-through' of the speech – making a few (tiny) amendments to language and remembering points of emphasis. The next stage could be a full run-through – standing up, on a stage if possible. It's best to have a small tripod for your smartphone so you can video this version, and try to get through the whole thing without stopping. If you're the adviser, take notes and resist the urge to interrupt. Then you can efficiently give feedback notes to the CEO and, if they want, watch the video back, pausing occasionally to make observations. (If watching themselves on video is likely to make the individual more nervous or self-critical, you should skip this bit. Most people, though, improve significantly once they see how flat and uninspiring their first take was.) Discuss points that could be improved, and go again. Repeat until your speaker leaves the room happy and fired up for the big moment.

If you've done enough prep work, a good rehearsal is sometimes the moment when the speaker's notes or scripts are thrown in the bin. When someone has rehearsed properly, the notes may not even be needed. The lead actor knows the part. Their veins are coursing with confidence. They are ready to take the stage.

Others will feel that, no matter how well they know their speech, however thoroughly they've rehearsed, they still need their cue cards. That's fine too.

Crush Nerves

The sweating. The wobbly legs. Feeling too hot. Feeling too cold. The racing heart. The dry throat. Ah, welcome back nerves, my old friends! You've threatened to spoil so many moments in my life. And yet you've also helped me get excited and properly fired up for the big occasions.

According to Robert Harris's account, Cicero – the great Roman orator – was sick before every important speech, so if you're tense before a big presentation or media interview, you're in very good company. In fact, I'd go as far as to say that if you're not nervous, you won't be a very good performer.

Leadership communication is – horribly and thankfully – riddled with fear. It's said that 90% of people are afraid of public speaking. The other 10% are probably lying.

If fear gets in the way of your ability to speak in public, the good news is that most people can find ways to manage it. We can have *less fear*. But we probably can't, and shouldn't, be *fearless*.

Every individual will have their own personal way of coping with nerves and beating them back. When I was at school, I auditioned one year to read a lesson at the Christmas carols in Westminster Abbey. It was a strange thing for a 14-year-old to want to do, but I suppose I wasn't your regular kid. I really wanted to read that lesson, wanted it so much that I was crippled with nerves for the audition. I could barely get the words out, I was shaking so badly.

I didn't get chosen. Nerves had beaten me. Since then I have treated nerves as my opponent in these situations. Either I win, or they do – and I simply can't let nerves win again and again and again. I've got to beat them. Smash them. Kill them. Use their fear to fire my anger – as a fighter and a competitor.

The next year, I went back to audition again and got to read the lesson in Westminster Abbey. And the year after that. And the year after that. I was, by then, taking lead roles in theatre shows and regularly getting up on the platform. I hadn't suddenly become an extrovert. In normal situations, I was notably shy. But I had become a performer.

So, my method is to have quite an aggressive fight with my nerves and see who comes out on top. This may not work for everyone. Many will want to welcome their nerves as good old friends and bringers of excitement. They'll want to think, *hey, the nerves have come to help me. They will allow me to deliver this with enough energy and enthusiasm.*

Towards the end of my TV reporting career, I often wasn't nervous *enough*. I would sometimes go on air with millions of people watching with scarcely a raised heartbeat. This is taking things too far in the other direction. My performances could occasionally be lethargic and poor. You need to be geed up. You need adrenaline. But it can't be out of control. A visibly nervous and uncomfortable speaker makes the audience nervous and uncomfortable. So what can you do?

- **Get out of your own head:** It's not about you; it's about the audience. You are not the hero; the audience is the hero. Focus on the material, not yourself. Think, *this is a gift to the audience. I am the bearer of the message. The message, though, is not me.* Switch your mental focus away from yourself and onto the people you're trying to reach. As Nancy Duarte, writer and CEO, says, "You're not Luke Skywalker. You're Yoda."[32]

- **Think, *what's the worst that can happen?*** It's just like the Dr Pepper adverts. Imagine the speech being an almighty catastrophe. Not only does the set fall down and you tip off the stage and break your neck, but the audience gets so angry that they throw things at you, smash your laptop and punch you. Oh, and then the whole building burns down. By imagining extreme disaster, the reality seems almost pleasant! Nobody dies. Most business speeches and interviews are rather dull. So mine can't be that bad.

- **Prepare:** Are you nervous because you haven't prepared or because you don't believe in the material? I'm at my best when I have been seriously nervous about a week ahead of something, and I've then spent a lot of time getting sorted. Honing and practising my material. Tightening things up. Rewriting and memorising sections. Then, on the day, there's often a beautiful serenity. Because I'm ready.

Then, of course, there are the physical things you can do to get ready. Actors will always do vocal and physical warm-ups ahead of a show. Reciting tongue twisters. Singing. Throwing balls around. Lying down. Breathing. Doing a few press-ups. Perhaps listening to music. Try it all and don't, ever, feel embarrassed about warming up properly.

However you do it, you must find a way of at least *appearing* calm and in control – even if you feel like a volcano. If you look anxious and stressed, your audience will become anxious and stressed.

One technique I've started to use is to watch videos of great talks, stand-up routines and motivational speeches before going on stage. By watching the top performers, I can get into the right frame of mind.

Make sure your diary is clear for *at least an hour*, and preferably the whole day, ahead of a big speech, presentation or interview. You need time to get into the zone.

---

[32] Nancy Duarte, on her website: www.duarte.com/great-presentations-the-audience-is-the-hero

PR for Humans practitioners prioritise the big moments, another of which is the MEDIA interview, the subject of the next chapter.

Summary

- **Clench and warm up:** You need to find stillness on stage, if possible. That's what will give you gravitas. Lower your centre of gravity by clenching buttocks and upper thighs. Pull a deeper voice out from within you. Ahead of time, concentrate on your clothes, hair and appearance. They are sending the most powerful signals.

- **The slides are not the speech:** You are the speech. *PR for Humans* is about *you*, not the presentation software. The slides, visual aids and (sometimes) props must support the story you are trying to tell. Only deploy them once you are clear about your idea and your argument.

- **Rehearse and prepare to beat nerves:** Sometimes you will want to memorise your speech, sometimes not. But you will always want to prepare thoroughly and rehearse properly. That's the best way to beat nerves.

3. MEDIA

What makes a good media interview? You've guessed it: the PR for Humans principles we outlined in Part 1.

Belief. Clarity. Opinion. Energy. Context. Time. Humility. Imagery.

Follow these principles carefully and you will already be in the top 1% of media performers. So what else do the practitioners of PR for Humans need to know?

This chapter explores the ongoing importance of media relations, and how business leaders should prepare for encounters with journalists.

Talk to Journalists

For much of the past 10 years, old-style PR (persuading journalists to publish your story) seemed to be slipping out of fashion. Why bother with newspapers and news programmes in the digital age?

Anyone could be a publisher. Anyone could make a video. The internet meant that companies and individuals were suddenly able to create and curate their own content channels.

All you needed was access to a smartphone and you could be an editor! You could write your own headlines! You could book yourself in for interviews! You never had to worry about being misquoted again!

Who needs the BBC, *The Financial Times*, *The Telegraph*, *The Times* and *The Wall Street Journal*? CNBC? Bloomberg? Reuters? Why bother, when you can reach your audience directly, though targeted digital storytelling?

There was a time, in the early days of blogging and social media, when it was a relatively open field. Anyone with a bit of imagination could set up a few social feeds and start to push their 'content' out there. It was easy to get noticed, to build a following, just by saying and doing interesting things.

PR directors, dependent for many years on their black books of connections with City and business journalists, were busy reinventing themselves as 'content producers', 'content marketers' and 'digital strategists' to enter the new communications gold rush.

Even the letters 'PR' vanished from most agency names, being as they were heavily associated with 'media relations' – picking up the phone to journalists and selling-in stories. Instead, those in PR learnt a new language of 'engagement' and 'social'. The best agencies found ways to grow their businesses in this new, democratic and chaotic world of communications.

James Gordon-Macintosh of Hope and Glory PR described it well on my *PR for Humans* podcast:

> The media when I 'grew up' in public relations in the 90s was pretty limited. You had a handful of papers and maybe 3–5 serious broadcasters. There has been an explosion of media opportunity now. It is, though, harder to have any impact. PR has had to get much better at having impact.

And there, of course, is the rub. We now live in world that is absolutely drowning in content. This new world of self-publishing is so easy, so cheap and so addictive that millions of people and millions of organisations are doing it. Nobody can possibly consume all the content that is now being pumped out.

The digitopia – the dream of bypassing traditional media and talking directly to your audiences – wasn't quite what it had seemed. As data flows increased exponentially, so it became harder and harder to get noticed. That's why the trusted news brands – such as the BBC, *The Financial Times*, *The Telegraph*, *The Times*, *The Wall Street Journal*, CNBC, Bloomberg and Reuters – are as important now as they ever were. Anything that features on their channels and editions has massive clout.

They have the power, through their reach and editorial credibility, to turbocharge stories. If they ignore you completely, your activities will be marginal. That may be fine if your objectives are very specific and modest. But if you want to make waves, you need 'the media'.

Digital communications and old-style media relations (contact with journalists) must now co-exist. If you generate coverage on trusted news sites, it will hugely enhance your digital profile. If you have great digital content, you will be much more likely to catch the eye of the journalists and secure coverage. Digital PR and traditional PR are both important for successful, high-impact communications.

Companies and individuals still need to talk to journalists if they want to be noticed and secure profile. The old tensions between reporters and PRs – hacks vs flacks – are as relevant as ever.

And for business leaders, the art of the media interview retains its critical importance.

Have a Goal for PR

There's got to be a point to any form of media engagement. It can't just be about vanity and coverage and profile and reach. The question with any form of media activity is: what you are trying to achieve?

You want PR, but why? What's the business goal? Perhaps you want to sell more products, increase brand recognition, attract the right employees or change government policy. Should you try to achieve these things through advertising or through influencing (e.g. public relations, where money doesn't change hands)?

Advertising is easier, but unless you have a big budget or some incredible ideas, 'pure PR' (i.e. media relations) will be more powerful.

Why? Because it has gone through an editorial filter. A trusted individual (a newspaper editor) has decided that you and your business are worth giving coverage to. This is many times more powerful than *paying* for column inches, airtime or social shares.

There is no effective PR without action. And we can't communicate the action unless we have a proper story. If communications people start talking about 'strategy', ask them very calmly what they mean by that. This is, I think, an area of massive confusion within the PR world.

A strategy is not a list of contacts or a grid of meetings. It's not a spreadsheet of 'deliverables'. Your strategy must be your overall plan which maps out where you want to get to and how you want to get there. *Strategy* will determine your focus and how you allocate resources. The *tactics* are the various things you will be doing along the way.

You can't, however, expect to win if you don't know what game you're even playing. If you want coverage because it makes you feel good, fine, be honest about it. But if you want your PR to deliver business value, then that will start with some proper thinking about the destination.

First decide the objective. Then find out as much as you can about the audience. Then find your story. Then consider tactics (and channels). No objectives that don't help business value. No strategy without a story. No tactics without effective channels. And you must always somehow measure the impact of all this activity.

The 'point of PR' is to deliver this and, importantly, get the order right. Not for the sake of vanity or ego, not to make happy clients, but for the benefit of the business or the career development of the individual.

That's *PR for Humans*.

Find Common Ground

Once you've worked out a proper strategy, then you can start to think about the individual engagements – the moments when you sit down and talk to reporters.

Here we arrive in the territory often described as 'media training'. In *PR for Humans*, media training begins with an explanation of the importance of finding common ground with the reporter.

You have a series of ideas and opinions that you want to impart – your circle. The reporter has angles they want to explore – their circle. The intersection of these two circles is where everyone is happy. You get good coverage. They get a good story.

It's surprisingly easy to find such common ground in a media interview, if you know what you're looking for.

The key to finding the common ground is knowing what the reporter is seeking *in advance* of the interview. This might be as simple as asking the journalist what their likely questions or headline could be. In the moments before the interview, you might find out what their thoughts are on the story.

Do everything you can to work out where their circle is. Then you can figure out which bits of your circle might overlap.

You need to think like a journalist, or hire someone who can think like a journalist, because successful media interaction comes down to an understanding not just of what you want to say, but what the audience is ready to hear. That means developing a sense of what is newsworthy.

Feel Newsworthy

Deciding what to put in 'the news' has always been notoriously tricky. In the end, it comes down to gut instinct and having the experience to hazard a guess at what audiences might need or want to hear. There's no magic formula, but there are a few questions that might help you stagger towards the answers:

- Is it new? Does the story contain things which we didn't know about yesterday/this morning?
- Is it significant? Does it directly affect a lot of people? If the answer is no, do we think a lot of people might worry that something similar might happen to them?
- Is there a character? Stories involving people we've heard about (celebrities, politicians, CEOs) are much more likely to get prominence.

- Does it form a pattern? Does the story build on other things that have happened recently?
- Is there conflict? Good stories usually have some tension or debate. If everyone agrees, the story fizzles out quickly.
- Is it bizarre? Sometimes the oddity value drives a story. Does it go completely against the grain of what we might think of as normal?
- Has someone been caught out? We might like to justify many stories in terms of the 'public interest' of exposing wrongdoers. *Schadenfreude* plays a big part. We (sadly) love reading about individuals who are falling from grace.
- Is there a strong human interest angle? Even if a story is insignificant according to the above questions, a strong emotional pull can trump everything.
- Are there good pictures? Again, great photos or a strong video sequence can outweigh much of the above.

These days, algorithms on social media platforms strongly influence whether a story is read, watched or shared. Powerful news brands like the BBC still play a key role, though, because we need someone to guide us through the endless thicket of digital content.

The above questions are still useful and relevant for those in PR and business to consider when trying to work out how to get a journalist's attention and generate some coverage. But the world has moved on from the insulated newsrooms in which I began my career in the late 1990s. In those days, editors would have the luxury of deciding the 'running order', without the distraction of a million tweets and posts. Fewer people these days sit waiting for the TV bulletin or the print edition of a newspaper or magazine.

Now, news is much more organic. It's a giant shape-shifter that looks different to each viewer depending on their vantage point, platforms and feed preferences. The professional journalists putting together their editions and programmes are all over Twitter, Facebook and a hundred other platforms. They themselves are hugely influenced by the waves and tides of digital comment. Their audiences are promiscuous and restless.

It's a mistake, though, to believe that old-fashioned editorial decision-making is no longer important.

It's also a mistake to think that news must become ever more immediate and shallow.

In recent years, there's been a reaction against the 'clickbait' of daft digital quizzes, sensationalist claims and silly videos. Modern audiences long for something more meaningful and intelligent. They have an unquenchable thirst, I believe, for more interesting material.

That's where the best common ground will be for you as a serious business leader – the most powerful intersection of your newsworthy opinions with the reporter's newsworthy angles.

Think like an editor. Think like a journalist. Ask whether those 'key messages' you've been handed are actually newsworthy. Think about your context. Step off your island. Ask whether that Q&A document that has been prepared is actually going to create a decent headline. Do you have an opinion that's worth repeating? Do you believe in the opinion? Can you deliver it with energy?

Write Your Headlines

Sometimes CEOs and business leaders complain that they have been misquoted or that the headline on the published article doesn't reflect what they wanted to say. To which my challenge is: "OK, what *did* you want the headline to be?"

They often don't have a clear idea. My attitude is that you can't complain about the reporter's angle if you're not sure yourself what the angle could or should be.

Preparation for a media interview begins with the question: what would I like my headline to be? If I opened the newspaper or online article, what might 'good' look like? What would I like to see as the finished article? Those in business who can visualise the desired outcome will have a much greater chance of getting the reporter to write it, or something similar.

But if you go into the media interview with 15 different things that you want to mention, the reporter will be confused. A confused reporter is a dangerous animal. They will start sniffing around for something juicier. A small section of your 30-minute conversation will be ripped out and consumed, without much thought about anything else.

So, visualise your desired media outcome. Think hard about what you'd like it to be.

Clarity.

Close your eyes. Imagine the headline you want to see. It can't be the type of thing a dictator would instruct his state-controlled media to publish. It can't just be 'Mike Sergeant is amazing' or 'Mike Sergeant triumphs again'.

With reporters we need to be subtle and, sometimes, a bit crafty in how we smuggle in the positive.

If you're a big-hitter, or your company is a serious market player, then the headline might be about you and your business. But if the reporter is to take the bait, you'll have to convince them that you're telling them something genuinely new. This might be a solid announcement (a deal, a hire, restructuring) or a shift in strategic focus. Either way, this is likely to be a significant moment for your business. You need in this instance to have given your desired headline a lot of serious thought.

In other instances, you are more likely to shape media by having a clear and memorable opinion. If you're a highly credible player, your opinion alone may be able to make the weather, or at least forecast it. Headlines could be of the form 'Sergeant predicts real estate revival' or 'Sergeant prepares for retail consolidation'.

You are more likely to create this type of headline if you are changing your position rather than just repeating it. Again, if you are a big player, this is likely to be a significant moment for you and your business.

If you're not important enough to make the weather, you can still secure important coverage by reacting to the headlines and forecasts of others. In this instance, you are voicing your view in the hope that the journalist will use your contribution to provide extra context and analysis.

It's still important to visualise the outcome and go into the media interview with a clear idea of what you'd like your quote to say. If you don't prepare, then prepare to fail.

So, work out your headline. Pre-write your desired quote. Go into the interview with that message beautifully polished and ready. Then make it irresistible to the reporter by crafting it into a soundbite.

Find Soundbites

Soundbites are short, succinct and memorable clips of between 10 and 15 seconds. I include this definition here because many clients (especially those outside the UK and the USA) aren't always familiar with the term.

Since the beginning of history, politicians and those in public life have been using soundbites (or their equivalent), but the term only entered the vernacular – via US politics – in the 1980s. As the news schedules became ever more crammed, reporters and producers would hack back speeches and interviews until the edited bursts were as tight and efficient as possible.

As Democratic candidate Michael Dukakis complained after the 1988 presidential election, *"If you couldn't say it in less than ten seconds, it wasn't heard because it wasn't aired."* [33]

Interestingly, that statement itself became a soundbite. This followed the use of another famous soundbite by his successful Republican rival, George Bush Snr: "Read my lips: no new taxes." [34]

In the 1990s, the soundbite culture reached its zenith in the UK with Tony Blair's rise to power: "Ask me my three main priorities for government and I tell you: education, education and education." [35]

Blair also, memorably, came up with the best soundbite at the time of the Good Friday Agreement in Northern Ireland by mocking the very concept: "A day like today is not a day for soundbites. We can leave them at home, but I feel the hand of history on our shoulders." [36]

As a TV and radio reporter, I loved soundbites. I used to spend hours watching interviews, speeches and debates, longing for the participants to say something – anything – that I could grab and put into a 15-second hole in my piece. So much that is said publicly is mind-achingly dull, so when the colourful, memorable burst comes, it's a wonderful gift to both the journalist and the audience.

Soundbites have a number of guises. These are some of the common ones:

- Metaphor – imagery, think 'hand of history'
- Clear commitment – think 'no new taxes'
- Strong opinion or call to action – think 'tear down this wall' (Ronald Reagan, 1987)

A good soundbite is pithy and taut, containing memorable, often visual language.

If you can deliver a good soundbite, in a speech or a media interview, the reporter is likely to find it irresistible to quote, or maybe even to use as the headline for the article. Particularly if everything else you say is plain.

"Ah, but what about authenticity?" I hear you ask. Aren't we fed up with politicians trying to shove their pre-prepared soundbites down our throats? Haven't we moved away from stage-managed, word-perfect delivery? Don't

---

[33] Michael Dukakis speaking to the *New York Times*, 22 April 1990.
[34] Speech by George H.W. Bush to the Republican National Convention, 18 August 1988.
[35] Speech by Tony Blair to the Labour Party Conference in Blackpool, 1 October 1996.
[36] Tony Blair statement to reporters in Belfast, 7 April 1998

modern audiences demand fluidity and flexibility? Don't we want our leaders to just *answer the question*? Yes, and no.

I have more in later sections on the return of longer-form content (podcasts and so on), and there's certainly a desire for particular audience segments to engage in unscripted, free-flowing conversation. Typically, however, this only reaches the super-fans and aficionados. If you want to connect with a wider audience, you must become a master of the short form.

It's certainly become harder to come up with powerful soundbites, and it's almost impossible to come up with good ones in spontaneous conversations. If you want to be witty, sometimes you've got to prepare! It isn't easy. So many of the formulations have been overused. So many of the metaphors are tired. That's why great soundbites are still so exciting.

Happily, if you come up with an original soundbite, you can use it again and again. Repeat it a few times, and people might just remember it.

Use a Story Tree

Those in the PR business are fond of a concept called a 'message house'. It's a useful way of cutting through complexity and simplifying communications. The idea is that you go into an interview with one big umbrella statement which sums up the main story you want to tell. This is the roof of your house. Supporting that statement are three pillars; they represent your three main messages in order of priority. Beneath those are the facts, figures and other proof points that you might need to support your argument; these are the foundations of the house. Fill in the message house and you have a clear framework for presenting your business to the world.

I have found the message house very useful at times. But it also has some limitations, in my view:

- The message house takes no account of the audience – these may be the things you want to show the world, but does anyone want to watch?
- The message house takes no account of the individual, the human being delivering the message. How does their story fit in?
- The house is a solid, fixed metaphor. It's not a growth metaphor. The rigid story doesn't easily change and develop.
- In the standard formulation of the message house, there is no reference to the all-important context – the themes in the market and the world that give you relevance and are critical for your communication.

So I've developed a possible alternative which I call the 'story tree'.

The roots are where you have come from (as an individual and a business) and the things that you care about and believe in. They are a representation of the past, but they also sustain and nourish you in the present – and the future.

Next is the trunk. This is your main, strong, powerful story. It supports your whole 'thing', whatever that is.

The branches are the different angles and opinions you may use in media interviews or conference speeches. They can grow and change over time, but they can't grow out of a completely different trunk.

The leaves are the show – the words, the images, the soundbites. They are the beautiful flourish. They are the colour and the rustle. They can also be renewed and refreshed with each season. The leaves must be things that the audience *wants* to see and hear, not just things you want to say and show.

Finally, I talk about the location and the weather. Where is the tree planted? In which country and market? What surrounds the tree? What other trees are nearby? The weather is also important, although of course it's changeable. This can include the economic climate, consumer confidence and the latest trends. This is what determines the all-important quality of *relevance*.

The story tree is my way of devising a strong and consistent story for a business and an individual that also allows for change and growth. An organic metaphor supports that.

This is the closest I usually come to what some in the industry call the corporate 'narrative'. Here's how a narrative process typically works:

1. Outline what's going on in the world
2. Define your company's strategy within that context
3. Paint a picture of the future – where it's all going

These can be useful staging points on the way to developing a story, but the problems with the standard 'narrative' are similar to the limitations of the message house. There is no reference to the audience. No account of the individual delivering the message. No potential within the framework to renew and grow.

I'm not dismissing either the message house or the narrative (although that's a very ugly word in business). Both are, at times, useful. These devices at least get you asking some of the right questions. They help with the distillation, and the search for clarity. Just don't forget to think about the audience and the things you care about most. Because in storytelling, you need to understand the *source* of your growth and the relevance for those you are trying to reach.

Broadcast Happy

I often ask my clients what makes them more nervous – print or broadcast interviews. Most say broadcast, without hesitation. The idea of going into a studio and sitting down in front of microphones and cameras is scary for many people, particularly if the programme is going out live.

You should certainly prepare thoroughly for a broadcast. Have real clarity about your headlines, and where the lines are that you mustn't cross. That said, studio appearances are usually very short. Your turn may feel massive to you, but it is just one short segment of hundreds, if not thousands of hours of TV and radio produced every day (millions of hours if you count YouTube and podcasts). In global terms, it's insignificant. So worry about it less.

The joy of broadcasting is also that what you say is what goes out – certainly on live shows. It's harder to be misquoted or taken out of context. It's far more nerve-wracking, in a way, to sit down with a print journalist for 45 minutes and have no idea which 20 words they might use as a quote, or what the headline might say.

TV can be a very superficial medium. I spent two years in the Middle East reporting on the intricacies of regional politics, religious divides and complex power struggles. When I returned to the newsroom, most people were only vaguely aware that I had been somewhere hot or dusty. And those are the people working in news. Goodness knows what – if any – impact my hours of TV analysis had on the mainstream audience.

So what then is the point of broadcasting? I think there are many good reasons for doing it. Sometimes, on prominent programmes, your contributions are picked up and circulated to a much wider audience. If you go on the Radio 4 *Today Programme*, your comments might well be re-reported by countless newspapers and blog sites. Broadcast is also your chance to be the figurehead, to show the world that you're a leader. Confident organisations and individuals are the ones sticking their hands up for broadcast opportunities. You want to be one of them.

Good broadcasting is about keeping things simple, using conversational language and just going for it with a bit of energy and attitude. People spend far too much time worrying about the questions they might get asked and not enough time geeing themselves up for what is, in effect, a little show. You are the performer. You are the entertainer.

Unless you are a politician or a naughty CEO, you will probably get a soft ride. The presenters and producers want you to perform well. They are on your side.

During a broadcast, you must look and sound like you are happy to be there, that you are enjoying your moment in the spotlight. The simplest and most effective performance trick is this: smile. Unless someone has died, just smile and lighten up a bit. Most contributors are way too flat and way too serious. Like it or not, the image you send out is critical.

If you are in the studio, look at the presenter and smile. The worst interviews are the ones in which the guest's eyes dart around, or they look like a rabbit in the headlights. Broadcast slots are over in a couple of minutes. Unlike print interviews (which stick around in digital editions), TV and radio appearances are done in a flash. Some video clips are posted on websites and social media, but most of the broadcast disappears into the electronic atmosphere. So use the moment. If you've got something to say, say it quickly. Or you might not get the chance to say it at all.

Broadcast (particularly television) is not a good medium for conveying facts, figures and lists of points. It is a good place to convey warmth, excitement, opinion and humour. Lots of people watch with the sound down in the office, or out of the corner of their eye at home. The impression you create – hopefully one of confidence and charisma – will be the main thing that is noted and remembered.

As with any of the other skills I've outlined, power and confidence flow from practise. The more you do, the better you get.

I was lucky in that I began my career working for an outlet that nobody watched! Reuters TV, a financial news channel, was transmitted directly into City dealing rooms. The traders and analysts turned the sound up when a news-making interview with a central banker or CEO was on, but I reckon my bits were mostly watched without sound. I could have been mouthing obscenities most of the time and I'm not sure anyone would have noticed. It was a glorious place to train. I was able to make any number of mistakes safely and anonymously, on air!

But how should others approach the DANGER inherent in public communication? The next chapter takes this up.

Summary

- **You still need to 'earn' coverage:** Despite the explosion in new ways to get your story direct to audiences via digital channels, editorial coverage remains a powerful determinant of reputation. *PR for Humans* must give journalists a story.

- **Find common ground with the reporter:** You've got to work out how your messages might intersect with the reporter's possible angles. To do that, you need to understand as much as you can about the journalist and the publication.

- **Build a story framework:** You need to work out what 'good' looks like to you. What is *your* desired headline? Could you express it in a crisp soundbite? Does the soundbite fit into the overall story framework that you've constructed for the business? Use a 'story tree' to build the elements you need to include in your version of *PR for Humans*.

4. DANGER

This section looks at how business leaders should cope with DANGER. How they can navigate the risks and pitfalls of media interviews and conference speeches. How they can stay safe while building profile and reputation.

Stay on the Record

Rule number one: stay on the record at all times.

Reporters will sometimes tempt you to go 'off the record', or to give them something which is 'on background' or 'non-attributable'. You might be at an event where what is discussed is under 'Chatham House Rules'. What do all these terms really mean?

Here's the theory:

- Off the record – nothing that is said can be quoted or attributed in any way
- On background – you can't report it directly, but the information can inform your reporting (a very hazy area)
- Non-attributable – the quote and the information can be used, but not the name or organisation of the person who said it
- Chatham House Rules – the information from an event may be reported, but the source may not be explicitly identified (again hazy if it's a public event with, say, only three speakers)

The reality is that the whole on/off the record thing is a very murky area. My advice is to leave it to the spin doctors and the masters of the dark arts. Unless you are in a very small group of people you have a trusted relationship with, it's very easy to come unstuck.

I never obtained any kind of formal journalism qualification, despite practising at the highest levels of the global industry for 18 years. The truth is that there is no international charter or universally accepted 'journalist code'. There are only courses – some good, some bad – and each reporter will have a slightly different approach to what exactly is 'on the record' and what isn't. And therein lies the danger.

You may have a clear idea about what is public and what is private information. The journalist may have a very different idea. Unless you know that individual well, it's best not to risk it.

So, to repeat my rule: stay *on the record* all the time (within reason). At events with 30, 40, 50 people, you are *on the record*. At a shareholders meeting, you are *on the record*. When you are with a reporter, you are *on the record*. And not just during the official 'interview', but throughout the meeting.

I sometimes warn CEOs and spokespeople about the 'Columbo moment', named after the fictional detective who, on his way out, used to say, "Just one more thing" as he delivered the question that snared the guilty killer.

Beware the moment when you think it's all over. The interview is finished. The notebooks, microphones and cameras have been put away. The interviewee relaxes and offers to show the journalist out. They are strolling back to the lift, when the reporter casually throws in a question which tempts the CEO to deliver an unwanted headline.

I've told clients about this. I've warned them in media training. But sometimes it still happens.

Not so very long ago, the CEO of a major bank had been lined up for an interview. He'd gone through the training. The agreement had been that this would be an interview about changes in the banking system. No political stuff, no Brexit nonsense, just real themes and issues in the industry. The interview went well. The reporter's notebook was closed. Then, when ambling to the lift, the CEO started talking about his contingency plans for Brexit. The honourable reporter knew he couldn't use the quotes directly, but within a couple of days, another two sources had stood the story up. Boom. Front page splash. Agony at corporate HQ.

So, leaders, stay on the record. It's not over till it's over. We're living in a very transparent, conscious world with paper-thin partitions and fragile data systems. The guidance has increasingly become: don't say anything or write anything to anyone that would cause you or your organisation major difficulty if it was all over a newspaper or website.

Stick to your messages and to the script. *The red recording light is always on.*

Watch Your Red Lines

Back at the end of the last century, I was conducting an interview with the Turkish finance minister for Reuters. I asked him whether he was considering abolishing an existing tax on shares.

"Yes. That's something we are considering," came the honest and straightforward reply.

The Turkish stock market went up like a rocket. That afternoon, around $16 billion was added to its value.

If he meant to say it, great. It was a nice use of using a trusted media source (Reuters) to get a credible message out. But I think the answer may have slipped out. He was asked a question and he answered it.

It could well have been a $16 billion slip of the tongue.

In media interviews, as well as preparing what you are going to say, you must also prepare what *not* to say. These are your red lines. Whatever happens during the interview, you can't cross your lines. Even if it means being boring. Even if it means you look evasive. Better that than generating an unwanted headline. The negative headline will stick. Boring gets forgotten.

These are some examples of common red lines that catch people out and are worth thinking about before a media interview or conference appearance:

- **Specifics:** If you are a politician, this could be the announcement of a tax/spending decision. For a business leader, it could be a decision on an acquisition, sale or the launch of a new service. Don't mention it before you are ready. It could destabilise the venture and/or kill media interest when you *are* ready to launch.
- **Clients:** Talking about your clients in public can bring a whole heap of problems. Some organisations have a strict 'no client mentions' policy, for fear of upsetting their paymasters. Better, if possible, to have some carefully curated client case studies that are ready for external use.
- **Competitors:** Again, think very carefully before calling out competitors live on air or on the conference stage. A public spat usually disadvantages both parties. If you want to go to war publicly, this needs to be part of a carefully worked out communications strategy. It can't slip out in the heat of the moment. In fact, better to praise your rivals in public than to seek to bury them.
- **Politics:** Yes, I encourage business leaders to have an opinion. But we do now live in an increasingly polarised political world.

Some of the fault lines are too big and the chasms beneath too dangerous. Work out where your political red lines are.

- **People:** Take great care when naming individuals. If you are saying nice things about them, it's usually OK. Public criticisms that get personal, however, risk creating unwanted reprisals and could even be libellous.

- **Mistakes:** If any of your past failures and misdemeanours are already in the public domain (however long ago), I advise you to have a form of words ready about them. Journalists are often lazy and will dredge things up that you thought had been settled long ago.

- **Company policy:** You may or may not be the CEO or senior leader, but be very careful about making up your company policy live on air (e.g. your view on a particularly contentious government issue or your record in promoting gender diversity or LGBT rights). In some interviews, you don't want to be drawn into these conversations unless you really know the answers and they've been agreed by the executive committee.

Every business will have different red lines. You may also have some personal red lines that you need to add to the company ones.

Ask yourself ahead of an interview: what's the worst that could happen? What might the most cynical, hard-bitten reporter ask here? Then prepare. These things will probably never come up. But if they do, you'll be much more assured when dealing with them.

Cut Down the Bridge

Don't you just hate it when politicians don't answer the damn question, but instead stuff their own messages into the interview? They don't sound like human beings. But *you* must. You've got to *speak human*.

Once you have identified your red lines, you should feel a lot more freedom in trying to listen to questions and answer them. That's what audiences want. They do not want an on-message robot, always trying to haul the interview back to the key points written out by the PR adviser.

The media training of the 90s and 00s became obsessed with the idea of 'bridging'. The leading practitioners even came up with what became known as the ABC method.

- **A – Acknowledge the tough question:** "I understand why you've asked that", "It's an interesting problem", "It's a good challenge".
- **B – Bridge:** Move across to the things you *do* want to talk about: "What's actually interesting to our clients...", "In fact the focus for us is...", "Can I just give you the context?".
- **C – Control:** This is where you are happily back on message: "The number one thing for us is...", "The key finding of our report is...", "The main thing we want to emphasise here is...".

This bridging method was also known as 'pivoting'. The reason it still gets taught is that people hire media trainers for one reason: to tell them how to stay out of trouble if they're asked a tough question.

For me, bridging can be ugly. I've rarely seen it done seamlessly and effectively. Far better – if you can – to be straight with people and talk like a human being. If you've identified your red lines, be straight about them:

- If you can't talk directly about clients, tell the reporter (ideally before the interview) that you can't talk directly about clients.
- If there are commercial sensitivities, tell the reporter (ideally before the interview) that some material is commercially sensitive, so you won't be able to comment.
- If you don't want to give political opinions, tell the reporter that you're a business strategist, not a political commentator.
- If you're asked a question about a controversy your company has been involved with, tell the reporter that you're not the spokesperson on that issue (unless you are the CEO or senior leader, in which case you will have to have a form of words ready).

It may be time to consign the bridge, the pivot, whatever you want to call it, to the dustbin full of outdated media training presentations.

Have interesting things that you want to say in media interviews. Go into the room with real excitement about your story and your ideas. Also, know what you *don't* want to say. Then just go for it.

If something completely unexpected comes up and creates an uncomfortable story then you probably didn't prepare your red lines well enough. Go back to the communications team, talk it through (without blame) and learn the lesson for next time.

But above all, have a story.

If you go into the interview with a story that resembles something the journalist might actually want to print or broadcast, it'll stop them nosing around for an awkward little angle.

So like Indiana Jones at the end of *Temple of Doom*, get out your sword and cut the bridge down! You probably won't need it.

Lean into Crisis

However well you craft your story and work out your 'red lines', there are moments for any business when something happens that blasts all your other plans and activities out of the water. A real crisis hits.

Whole books have been written about dealing with crises. Entire agencies have been set up purely to help businesses respond to and recover from disaster and calamity. A crisis can be very complicated. But the principles of effective crisis management from a human PR perspective are simple. They can be summarised in this small section.

The first thing you need to do is try to expect the unexpected. The former US defence secretary Donald Rumsfeld famously put it like this in 2002:

> There are known knowns; there are things we know we know. We also know there are known unknowns; that is to say we know there are some things we do not know. But there are also unknown unknowns – the ones we don't know we don't know.[37]

There was much amusement at the time. This quote seemed to sum up the weasel-worded obfuscation of the 'War on Terror' period between the 11th of September 2001 and the invasion of Iraq in 2003. But Rumsfeld had a point.

There are three types of situations: the ones we can predict, the ones we can imagine but can't predict, and the ones we can't imagine or predict. Businesses should spend quite a bit of time and effort thinking about the first two.

A proper crisis-preparedness process scans the horizon for issues that might explode at some point. It then tries to imagine worst-case-scenario events that could happen, even if the way in which they may play out is hard to foresee with accuracy. These could be a mixture of the personal and the organisational. Embarrassing and genuinely tragic. Examples might include:

---

[37] Donald Rumsfeld, Pentagon briefing: www.youtube.com/watch?v=GiPe1OiKQuk

- Your data files are hacked and information relating to your entire client roster is compromised
- An accident takes place at one of your facilities, involving the tragic loss of life of employees and/or customers
- A member of your staff does something seriously harmful or offensive to customers or members of the public
- A senior individual (maybe even the CEO) is caught out for corruption, a sexual misdemeanour or other deviance

Smart comms people put in place plans to tackle these hypotheticals long before any actual event occurs. The most important thing you need at these times is a structure.

When unexpected and serious things happen, the UK government has COBRA meetings (named after Cabinet Office Briefing Room A, where the crisis team assembles). You don't necessarily need to christen a meeting room, but you do need to know what the chain of command is in a crisis. Who is in the inner circle? Do you have mobile numbers for everyone in one place? Can you easily set up an email or WhatsApp group to coordinate your response?

Crisis-preparedness sessions can be simple or complex. You might test responses in a room, just as a basic workshop. Or you might invite a firm in to simulate a full, screaming calamity complete with pretend video clips, fake tweets and imaginary press releases. It's entirely up to you.

Paul Blanchard is a PR consigliere who works exclusively with global CEOs. He told me what his advice is to those in a seriously sticky situation.

"Reputations can shatter within a couple of hours. Huge global brands can be affected. But the one thing they do have control of is how they respond," he said on the *PR for Humans* podcast.

"In any situation, you're like a pizza shop manager. The order has been taken down wrong. The customer is upset. It's not your fault. You didn't personally take the order down. You didn't cook the pizza. But you have to respond.

"You have to lead on empathy. Say, 'I'm terribly sorry'. It is not about you. It's about showing that you understand the customer. Next, you take responsibility. It's not your fault, but you say, 'I'm taking responsibility for this'. Thirdly, you promise to put it right."

Lead on empathy. Take responsibility. Promise to put it right.

Paul's formula is a great 1, 2, 3 for crisis handling.

Show the customer that you get why they're upset/angry. Show that, despite the fact that you are not personally responsible, you are taking this problem on your shoulders. Show that you are doing everything you can to sort it out and ensure it won't happen again.

When the crisis hits, *it's not about you*. It's always about the people directly affected by whatever almighty screw-up your firm has been involved with. But at that moment you – as the CEO and the leader – must be there. Be present. Be visible. Show the world that *this and only this* is commanding your complete attention.

When a business leader does this, most people out there will say, "Fair enough. He/she is doing what they can". The crisis passes.

There is, however, a strategic judgement to be made in all of this, as to how much media the CEO/leader does in the heat of the moment. A series of TV interviews can fan the flames of disaster, quickly turning a little incident into a full-on meltdown. If millions of customers are affected, you need to get out to the broadcast studios quickly, but don't broadcast for hours on end. Do a quick round of interviews and move on. If the 'crisis' only affects 10 clients, don't go near the media; call the clients directly or get them in a room.

But whatever media response you decide on (full megaphone or under the radar) the approach remains: lead on empathy, take responsibility and promise to put it right.

Sometimes, the best way to regain control of your story is to start to produce more of your own CONTENT, which is where we're heading next.

Summary

- **Stay 'on the record' at all times:** Treat every interview and conference appearance as a live situation. The boundaries aren't clearly defined. Unless you know and trust the reporter, assume that anything you say may be used.

- **Work out your red lines:** Brainstorm the toughest, most awkward and challenging questions in advance. Instead of trying to bridge away from them in an awkward, robotic way during the interview, figure out how to answer or block those questions before you get into the room. Speak like a human being.

- **Take responsibility for a crisis:** When disaster strikes, show your human side. Sympathise and empathise first. Then assume command and responsibility. Promise to do everything in your power to stop it happening again.

5. CONTENT

This chapter looks at CONTENT – how business leaders should approach videos, podcasts and photography in the context of a world dominated by the swirling power of social media.

Belief. Clarity. Opinion. Energy. Context. Time. Humility. Imagery.

The PR for Humans principles will determine the power of your content, whether it's made for your own website or shared on other platforms.

When making and packaging our own stories, we've got to think about human audiences at every stage. Ask: how can we make this meaningful for real people?

Let's start with video.

Get Video

On the 14th of February 2005, a new internet domain name was activated. It was called YouTube.com.

The previous year, two things happened that accelerated the demand for a global video-sharing platform. One was a disaster on a biblical scale. The other was a comically memorable celebrity blooper.

The first incident was the Asian tsunami. The second was Janet Jackson's unfortunate 'wardrobe malfunction', when her breast popped out during her performance at the Super Bowl. YouTube co-founder Jawed Karim says he couldn't easily find video clips of either event online. The idea for an easily searchable video-sharing site was born. YouTube opened its first office above a pizza restaurant in San Mateo, California.

A year and a half later, YouTube was acquired by Google for over a billion dollars. Ten years later, the platform reached another significant 'billion' – for the first time, *1 billion hours* of YouTube videos were watched in a single day. That's an hour of YouTube watching for every seven people on the planet. Putting that into perspective, if you were to sit down personally and watch 1 billion hours of video, it would take you over 100,000 years. That's longer than the whole of human history.

And online video is just getting started.

This explosion of video has turned the communications world inside out and on its head. If, like me, you grew up in an era of highly produced, expensively crafted film and television, the junk-filled expanding YouTube universe can feel like a frighteningly vast and careless space. But it's also brought about a cornucopia of learning, entertainment and business opportunities.

Chris Roberts, former Sky News correspondent and now owner of Invision Communications, says that, pre-YouTube, only a handful of CEOs were using video. Now it's hard to find a single chief executive who isn't getting something filmed on a regular basis. This is what he told me on the *PR for Humans* podcast:

> Ten years ago, you'd have the CEO sitting behind a desk or by a roaring log fire in their country estate. They'd go: 'Well hello everybody, I'd like to talk to you about how much money *I'm* making – err... *you're* making... err... the company is making'. That just doesn't cut it anymore. You need to be a storyteller. You can't just stand in a boardroom. You need to tell a story in a way that's colourful, engaging and impactful.

The indulgent corporate videos of the past – with stirring music, sweeping zooms and luxurious pans – have been largely swept away by the YouTube culture. If a video-gamer can make millions making videos in their bedroom, then a global CEO sitting there all stuffy and presidential can look like the most buttoned up and remote figure imaginable. That doesn't mean that business leaders should start doing dozens of video selfies in their pyjamas. There's still, thankfully, a place for high-end content. And there's also a case for the grab-and-shoot videos that capture the moment.

"If I'm a CEO who is announcing a billion-pound merger with another company," says Roberts, "I don't want to do a video on an iPad that looks as if the dog's paw hit the record button. It sends out the wrong message. However, if I'm that same CEO and I've just run the marathon with my team to raise money for the company charity, to have a 10-second video recorded on a smartphone with my arm around other members of staff, looking exhausted but triumphant – that is more effective and powerful than inviting a 4K film crew to capture the moment you've crossed the finish line."

Good business video strikes the right balance between formal (highly produced, well edited, properly shot) and informal (of the moment, authentic, emotional). CEOs fail when they go too far in either direction on the wrong occasion. Video, like all other modes of communication, has also become much more of a conversation. If you think you can sit in your office up on the 11th floor and broadcast out to your minions, then your videos will arouse distrust and resentment. They will also fail if they're too long, pompous and self-indulgent. You've got to allow your viewers the chance to engage and interact.

If 10,000 employees worldwide are told to watch a half-hour CEO video, that will waste 5,000 hours of company time – an absurd brake on productivity. But regular, colourful videos that engage, inspire and show a different side of the company are fabulous for morale and cement a culture faster than anything else.

Here's the good news for the CEOs who don't like appearing on camera: the best videos probably won't feature you at all. You need to do everything you can to find human stories across your organisation *at every level*. Maybe the security guard has an interesting backstory. Maybe the guy in the accounts department is a painter in his spare time. Perhaps the new graduate has an interesting story about what she did in her year out in Africa. Find those stories. Film them. Focus on your people.

You can use videos for a much broader range of moments and events than might have been possible in the past, because they are so much cheaper these days. Think well beyond the usual video about company results or the annual presentation. Make a little video to launch a new office. Cut one to celebrate a milestone. Commission one for a significant new product. You need to be able to make them quickly, with minimum 'process' and maximum agility. Don't stress it. Don't edit out all the fun. Find the strange, the interesting and the unexpected. Look – *always* – for the human stories. Find the people in your business who can bring it to life.

Use video to break down barriers, not build them. Use video to celebrate the full diversity, vitality and all-round awesomeness of your business. Make the films snappy, short and full of fun.

When it comes to video, just get over yourself! A video is never complete. It's never the whole answer. It's never a comprehensive summary of the year. It's just a taste of something that's going on.

This is what I've been telling myself too. If there are more than 1 *billion* hours of video watched on YouTube every single day of the year, your little piece to camera is a speck of dust in the solar system.

Make it colourful.

Podcast Around the Campfire

Long before the first humans started writing things down and preserving their texts, communication existed as oral tradition. Knowledge, art, ideas and cultural references were passed on through speech and song. Folktales, ballads, chants, prose and verses were transmitted and refreshed through performance. Sometimes the stories would be acted out, but often they would be audio experiences. Civilisation developed in the medium of sound and voice.

As BBC reporters, we were schooled in the purity of radio, as opposed to the less subtle medium called television. On radio, we connect in a deeper way with the personality of the presenter and the guests because we are not distracted by lots of shiny things flashing in front of our eyes. We can *hear the stories*. They seem to have greater resonance and meaning. Radio is a wonderful way of conveying warmth, emotion and trust. Deep and lasting bonds can be built with listeners.

One example of this is the experience of any new editor of the BBC's *Today Programme* on Radio 4. Even tiny changes to the established running order, like moving 'Thought for the Day' from its cherished 07.45 slot, brings howls of outrage from the programme's devoted army of listeners. They love the routine, the rhythms of the show and the familiar personalities. Tinker with the formula at your peril.

When I entered journalism in the late 90s, however, it was assumed that radio was in dignified and graceful decline and would increasingly struggle for audiences alongside its younger and flashier visual cousins. The TV and video streaming services seemed to offer more compelling and complex storytelling opportunities. But radio has not only defied its doomsayers, it has steadily increased its reach in the UK. And now – with the podcast – a new, less structured, less controlled but more democratic world of radio has burst onto the digital airwaves.

Podcasts have been around since I was covering the rise of the internet during the dot-com boom. You could sit at your computer and play audio files. However, two developments have super-charged the podcast and dragged this online side hustle into the centre of the media marketplace. Firstly, the explosion in smartphone use and 4G means you can now stream audio on the move; you don't have to download audio files or listen to them on a desktop. Secondly, the rise in streaming platforms like iTunes and Spotify has brought podcasts within a thumb click for anyone with a decent signal.

And yet, for years, I remained a podcast sceptic. Who's got time to listen to hour-long audio shows? In a typical day, we're dividing our attention into 30-second bursts. A minute of video sometimes seems like a commitment. The key, I now realise, is to consume stories and information *while doing other things*. Cooking the dinner? Stick on a podcast. Walking the dog? Podcast. Running? Podcast. Commute? Podcast. It's like attending an interesting lecture or event in these otherwise empty mental spaces.

Podcasts are becoming increasingly important for business communication because they allow companies to reach and curate niche audiences of super-fans and influencers. Even if the show only has 100 listeners, that's the equivalent of doing an event in front of 100 people every week. And it's a lot cheaper and easier to produce.

"I call it the audio of the campfire," said Richard Miron, former BBC correspondent and communications expert at the UN and the World Bank, who now runs a podcasting business called Earshot Strategies. Speaking on the *PR for Humans* podcast, he continued:

> The opportunity to reach niche groups – whether they are professional or personal – and share ideas. The fact that you can do it without a transmission mast. I feel very strongly about it. It drove me to set up this consultancy. This was the lightbulb moment for me. Creating the audio campfire. Unlike videos, podcasts are not expensive to produce. It's a potent medium when combined with technology. For business, it allows them to talk to customers, stakeholders and employees directly.

But, as Richard emphasises, the podcasts you create must have editorial integrity. They've got to be intelligent, relevant broadcasting. They can't just be marketing brochures. Done well, they can give a voice to all sorts of people who otherwise might not get heard. The conversations, though, must be interesting. You've got to give your listeners something that takes their thinking in a new and unexpected direction. Podcast listeners are usually obsessive learners. They develop and grow through audio. They want to hear emotional and honest stories of people who've struggled and overcome challenges. They want those lessons in their pods.

In business, you should be investigating how best to use podcasts to reach and engage your audiences – be they investors, regulators, staff, partners or new recruits. But try to make it as democratic and inclusive as you can. That's the joy and power of the medium. Beware the 'view from the 11th floor' podcast, in which the CEO delivers a monologue about how successful he/she is. Make the podcast a wider and more diverse experience. Talk to people at all levels of the business. Talk to people outside the business.

I started off doing a podcast about PR by talking to comms people, but soon realised this was very limiting. Far better, I decided, to do a podcast for communicators, but featuring a diverse and eclectic range of contributors, including comedians, actors, novelists, illustrators, digital content creators and all sorts of other people who are trying to reach audiences in myriad ways. Much of the material has found its way into the pages of this book, and I hope it's a much better book because their stories have pushed my own thinking in new directions.

The audio of the campfire works best when you can assemble like-minded and interesting people around that fire for the conversation. As the host of a podcast, you've got to be a contributor as well. You need to give the audience your personality – the quirks, the humour, the struggles, the emotions. At the beginning (and maybe forever) it will feel experimental, and somewhat scary. But that's the joy of the podcast. It's a new world of audio with no rigid rules on structure, length or style. You can make it up as you go along, and *nobody cares.*

It is the joy of an interesting conversation where you discover something new and connect with a stranger.

As we all know deep down inside, audio has a timeless power to inspire, persuade and educate. Use it, in some way.

Find Photo Beauty

"Photography is what I think about last thing at night and first thing in the morning. It's a form of therapy. It's helped me recover from a series of what might in the past have been called nervous breakdowns," said Chris Booth, a friend and colleague who I first met at Associated Press Television (APTV) in 1997.

Chris and I also worked together for the BBC in Baghdad in 2007/2008 during the peak of the post-invasion conflict in Iraq. It was a time of senseless, mind-draining violence. We were cooped up in the BBC house, a guarded compound across the river from the Green Zone, where the Americans, British and Iraqis had their main operations. Occasionally we would go out on brief forays to parts of the city in an unmarked van to gather some material or jump on a helicopter to 'embed' with US troops somewhere. For the most part, we relied on brave Iraqi journalists who would go out on our behalf and be our eyes and ears on the ground.

Chris came to photography in a serious way a few years later, after he'd left the BBC and moved into communications roles, firstly with the European Bank for Reconstruction and Development (EBRD). I was interested in how someone who'd spent most of their career in television and radio news, sometimes in extremely difficult and dangerous locations, could have settled on photography as the most meaningful – and, for him, therapeutic – medium. This is what he told me on the *PR for Humans* podcast:

> I think photography gives you a sense of perspective, but more important than that... a sense of beauty. We don't talk about beauty very much, although I believe we can all feel its presence. Being able to frame the world in a way that is pleasing – that goes to the heart of it.

Images are central to any kind of storytelling, as we have already discussed – whether verbal or purely visual. The power of the photograph is, according to Chris, that the person looking at it can *in their own time* find the meaning and discover the story. Contrast that with video, where the director or editor decides the tempo and duration of the viewing experience. There's also the efficiency and precision of the picture:

> Images can economically convey a range of meaning and emotion at one go that would take reams of writing to accomplish. And meaning and emotion, conveyed clearly, are at the heart of good communications.

Rarely in PR or communications do people talk about the storytelling power of photographs. Too often the corporate 'stock shots' or bland 'headshots' take up space on websites and documents that could be used for much more impactful and meaningful storytelling. Digital technology, smartphones and Instagram mean everyone is now a photographer and publisher. Our lives are lived out in photographs. And yet, great photographic storytelling is surprisingly rare in professional 'corporate' communications.

Worse than a missed opportunity, so much photography is in fact *damaging* to the story that the person or the business is trying to tell, according to Chris. We are an increasingly sophisticated audience. Badly chosen images or images that are retouched badly are a real risk. People want authenticity. Cheese isn't tolerated, unless it's highly ironic, self-aware cheese.

A clichéd image risks more harm to your message than clunky prose. Skimping on strong photography has a cost. It can make you look inauthentic, superficial and lacking in judgement. As we scan websites, our eyes lock onto the pictures before the words. The photo, in many cases, holds the key to the rest of the content, which will be overlooked or ignored if the image is weak, or jars with the story that is being told.

But, Chris emphasised to me, you need to do things the right way around. To tell a story with pictures, you need a story to tell in the first place. Get that straight first, before hiring photographers.

As we finished the podcast recording, the conversation turned to the often awkward transition from the world of journalism to the world of PR. Sometimes this is called crossing over to the 'dark side'. I like to turn that on its head. Journalism is the darker realm for sure, obsessed as it is with things going wrong: death, disaster, scandal, resignation, misfortune. PR is the lighter place. Seeing the world through a positive lens isn't a bad thing, particularly if, like Chris and me, you have seen some of the worst pain that human beings can inflict on one another.

But there is an important similarity between good journalism and *PR for Humans*. It is the centrality of storytelling – *by* people and *for* people.

"Honesty is still valuable. Beauty is appreciated. Truth is still meaningful," said Chris.

I agree. That is a thought to hold onto. And to share.

Get Human on Social

That brings us to social media. Whole agencies and international businesses are built on advising on 'social strategy'; armies of 'digital consultants' patrol the corridors of global corporations preaching the gospel of 'sharable content'. Even to experienced communications professionals, social media can seem like a swirling vortex of space garbage.

In their personal lives, many humans try to find ways to cope with #social – even though we haven't properly evolved and adapted for it. Many others shut it off and close it down completely. But love it or loathe it, the Twittersphere, Facebook timeline and Instagram feed are important (some might say, completely dominant) features of the communications universe.

For years, the whole of the advice industry was built on the premise that the purpose of social media was to post and exchange original 'content'. But that's only part of the story. Content – even excellent content – doesn't generate the social returns on its own anymore, if it ever did. A 'content strategy' must be replaced, or more likely enhanced, with an 'engagement' plan. Users must find ways of interacting properly with others via social media and responding to *their stuff*. That's the only way it works to provide any sensible value. There's simply too much content for followers to be able to evaluate it meaningfully on its own merits. Successful social animals are the ones who can hook their audiences in a split second with something visual, outrageous, shocking or provocative *and then engage with them.*

Some businesses have a very strong brand identity that audiences know and respect, so their social media can work as a distribution channel for material that is already likely to be valued. For other businesses, social media is a very hard place to establish a brand and build a foothold. Success comes down to having something to say *and* responding to the things others have to say. This is time consuming, risky and often frustrating.

It's also a world of heightened tension, ramped-up emotion and shallow opinion. Often it resembles a vast echo chamber of distorted information particles bouncing off the walls and colliding at frightening velocity. It seems to bring out the best and (more often) the worst of humanity. It's a tough place to try to build influence in any sort of sensible, methodical way.

And yet.

In business, we can't shut social media off. We can't press the Luddite button. We can't create a digital-free utopia. To survive and have any impact, we must learn to use it and to manage it. Somehow.

For a long time, as a journalist, adviser and consultant, I was scared of social media. I needed a view on it but didn't feel like I understood it well enough. The thing I came to realise is: there is no 'it'. Social media has no identity. At best, it's a platform. *It doesn't care.* The debate rages about whether Facebook and others should have the responsibility of publishers and have more editorial control. The fact that they don't take much editorial responsibility is terrifying. But maybe the thought that they might take more editorial responsibility (and actively decide what the whole planet should see) is even *more* terrifying.

For business leaders, I believe this is what it comes down to: all social media does is put a spotlight on humanity. As Molly Flatt, author and tech journalist told me on the *PR for Humans* podcast:

> People are still people. We are very arrogant if we think our digital tools can change them. We thought the digital tools were going to build the utopia for us. We forgot we had to play very close attention to the design and the storytelling. Social media is a very personal thing. All it does is expose and amplify who you are.

This makes social media for a *business,* a *company* or an *organisation* very difficult to get right. At best, social media is the expression of the human story. It's very hard for *organisations* to have a decent human story. If they do, it's tied up with the story (or stories) of the founder/CEO and other principal characters, or it is very focused on the customer as a human being. And the most effective people on 'social' are the ones who already (perhaps unknowingly!) follow the *PR for Humans* principles: belief, clarity, opinion, energy, context, time, humility and imagery.

Is this Social media *for humans*? Yes. In many ways. That's good and bad. It's both a force for positive human good and an agent of the dark side of human nature. You can, for sure, create movements and build influence on social. In fact, these days you've probably got to try. But don't think any fancy 'digital tools', 'follower apps' or 'influencer mapping solutions' are going to do all the work for you. They might help to point you in roughly the right direction, but then it's down to you. You, the human being. You need things to say and stories to tell. Your real character will ultimately be the thing that matters. Oh, and persistence. And a bloody thick skin.

We thought our technology was building a new world, but that world is populated by the same humans – with all their brilliance and maddening flaws.

And in this digital world, WORDS still matter, as we shall see in the final chapter of *PR for Humans*.

Summary

- **Use video to break down barriers:** Filming the CEO talking from on high can create a massive barrier between them and the audience. Instead, use video to celebrate human diversity and explore different points of view.

- **Embrace audio:** It has a timeless power to persuade and educate human audiences. Always focus on making podcasts as interesting as possible in their own right. Don't seek to push your messages or agenda into them too obviously.

- **Use beautiful photos:** They remain a very efficient way of conveying meaning and emotion, and yet they are often ignored by those in PR. Find a story first, then use a photographer to bring depth and meaning to the story. Avoid the corporate stock shots – they are the road to communications perdition.

- **Converse on social media:** It's more about engagement than content. There's little point posting without interacting. Cutting through on social is about being human. This is often difficult for organisations to understand.

6. WORDS

Polonius: What do you read my lord?

Hamlet: Words... words...words.[38]

Our final chapter explores how we can find more impact in business with our WORDS. We will look at the secrets of good writing and examine how we can use writing to engage our audiences more quickly and effectively.

How do we make our words work?

Belief. Clarity. Opinion. Energy. Context. Time. Humility. Imagery.

Writing, too, follows the PR for Humans formula. Now let's see how to put it into action.

Write Clearly

The most impressive political and business leaders I've worked with are usually clear and effective writers. Often, people will talk about 'good' writing and 'great' writing. What I've learnt over the years in business and communication is that the quality we really seek is 'clear' writing.

There are those with poetry in their soul, who can produce a nice turn of phrase. There are those who can craft intricate sentences and use words to create a piece of art on the page. These are wonderful skills. But most of the time, in business and in life, we simply need to be able to write quickly and efficiently and clearly.

When I graduated, I wasn't a particularly skilled writer. As with anyone who'd spent years in academic institutions, my writing was overcooked. There were too many adjectives and adverbs. When I went serious, there was far too much detail. When I went flowery, it was pretty LSD.

My early news scripts at APTV got the whole newsroom chuckling, particularly when I was assigned to cover London Fashion Week. Here was

---

[38] *Hamlet* by William Shakespeare, Act 2 Scene 2.

the 22-year-old economics graduate with zero fashion sense trying to write scripts to describe the coolest models and craziest catwalk creations. My writing went off into orbit, with the most colourful and outrageous prose I could muster. The editors should have hauled me aside for the extravagant nonsense I was producing. But everyone, myself included, was having far too much fun with those scripts. So, whenever a fashion story came along, I was asked to give it the 'Mike Sergeant treatment'. I cringe now to think of it.

The problem most graduates have is that they are used to producing academic essays. There's an introduction which sets up the argument. Then either side of the debate is explored. Finally, we meander our way towards the conclusion, itself often stuffed with caveats. This isn't how people write in business. The best professionals write for action. It's not about conveying knowledge or facts. It's not (usually) the place to weigh up arguments. The reader wants to go straight to the action point. The conclusion usually comes first.

The business reader doesn't have time. They want to stop reading as soon as possible. The document or email needs to tell them why they are reading this and what they need to do about it. No introduction. No debate. The conclusion – if anything – is the opening paragraph. If they want more information or context they can carry on with the rest of the text.

The essential elements of a story were first set down by the Greek Hermagoras of Temnos, a Greek rhetorician of the Rhodian school and teacher of rhetoric in ancient Rome. He divided a topic into seven questions:

1. Who?
2. What?
3. When?
4. Where?
5. Why?
6. In what way?
7. By what means?

The last two were dropped for being too wordy, and the Hermagoras formula became the 'five Ws' – used now in every journalist college and police training academy. Those five questions need to be answered if you're to make any progress with a news story or any kind of investigation.

If you write an email or an article, we need to know very quickly WHO it is about, WHAT has happened, WHEN it happened, WHERE the action is and WHY it happened. In business, I think we need to add another question to the five Ws: how do we fix it?

Business people are problem-solvers. They are the people who overcome obstacles and get stuff done. This is the difference between the business scribe and the hack. Reporters can, as I did for many years, stand on the sidelines and tell the audience what is happening. But the leader of a business can't be a passive spectator. They must be in the action, with a fistful of solutions.

As my reporting career developed, my writing improved in some ways. I got more efficient. My sentences got shorter. I dropped the flowery prose (most of the time). I tried not to use words that were not widely understood. I tried to write as if I was speaking, or could be speaking, the text. If I have a style now, it's that of a broadcaster.

No, I am not and never will be a *great* writer. But, often under immense pressure, I've had to become a fast and efficient writer.

As a TV reporter, I would sometimes write the final lines of a news report five minutes before the item was due to be broadcast to millions of people. That's no time for writer's block. With a gun pointing to your head, you've got to spit out some phrases or it's over.

My advice to people in business: you are not usually writing to entertain. You are mostly writing to convey information, opinion and action.

Clear writing reflects clear thinking.

In fact, I would go further. Clear thinking is impossible without writing. When you start setting words down on the page, you find out what you think.

Writing is the route to clarity – in your own mind, if nothing else. And with clarity, everything is possible.

But you'll almost always have to go back and edit and edit and edit.

Rewrite Everything

By rewriting our articles, speeches, blogs and books, we can get a little closer to the clarity and energy we seek. Usually we need to strip things down, take things out, move bits around and smooth the edges.

A sentence is rarely improved by an extra descriptive word. 'Adjectives and adverbs rarely add anything', goes the saying. Set aside the pedantic constructs and elaborate flourishes. Replace long-winded discursive paragraphs with the language of action. Write active rather than passive sentences. Use a conversational style – the way we speak in normal, everyday interaction.

If you wouldn't say it, don't write it. Cross it out.

To do *PR for Humans*, you've got to write as humans speak and as humans like to be spoken to. Sometimes I think we get into difficulty because the computer programs we use (for emails, documents and spreadsheets) are just too darned good at remembering facts, words and information. It's so easy to copy and paste chunks of writing. Sentences, paragraphs, whole pages can be reproduced with the click of a mouse. We don't stop to question: would a human being ever actually say these words on the page?

So, to get to the point, here is my writing checklist:

- Use shorter rather than longer words. Never use a word on paper that you wouldn't use in conversation.
- Go through every sentence and ask: can I remove any jargon? Is there a simpler, more everyday way of saying that?
- Use shorter sentences. Rip out the sub-clauses. Write in bursts. Sometimes entirely verbless. Usually nobody complains.
- Paint pictures, either by vividly describing real things or by using metaphors that hook the mind's eye.
- Use alliteration sometimes, if you want to **p**resent and **p**erform **p**owerfully.
- Use repetition. I mean it. Use repetition. It gives emphasis. It's stupid, but it works. Say it. Repeat it. Repeat it in the middle. Repeat it again at the end.
- Use rhetorical questions: "Is it too late for companies to act?", "How can we solve such a complicated problem?", "Why aren't most investments delivering?"
- Use contrasting pairs – the oldest trick in rhetoric: "You can take the easy road, or the more challenging route", "You can enjoy change, or you can fear it", "Success requires investment and foresight. If you fail to invest, your failure becomes certain".
- Use groups of three: 'triads'. You can either repeat a phrase three times, or have three parts to a statement:
  - ▷ "I came. I saw. I conquered." (Julius Caesar)
  - ▷ "Education. Education. Education." (Tony Blair)
  - ▷ The good, the bad and the ugly
  - ▷ Life, liberty and the pursuit of happiness

OK, that's the technical stuff over.

Some of the most useless and boring books ever written are by the pedants of 'good writing', with their rigid rules on grammar and 'style'. If you want to ignore the rules/advice above, that's fine by me. Just keep things clear and conversational. Convey opinion and action. Always look at the context. Try to write visually. And, when you can, go a little deeper...

Write from the Gut

But how do you go deeper?

You can write from the heart, the head or the gut. Effective communication requires all three, to some degree.

Your heart gives you the emotional connection to the material and to the audience. Your head allows you to produce a coherent and logical argument. But to really punch through, you also need to bring your gut into the story.

Richard Skinner is a novelist and director of the fiction programme at Faber Academy, which runs a celebrated six-month 'Writing a Novel' course. It has produced some of the best debut novelists of recent years. When I met Richard in Bloomsbury, I was keen to find out more about his views on storytelling. This is what he told me on the *PR for Humans* podcast:

> Good writing comes from a very deep place inside you. It comes from the stomach. You can be too much in love with your novel or overthink your novel. The best writing is from the gut. You have to have a good gut feeling for a story... you have to care about what you are writing. It's got to bother you. It's got to bother you so much that you have to get it out.

I think this applies to non-fiction as well as fiction.

Most business writing is all head and no heart or gut. But as humans, this isn't how we like to consume stories. We bore easily with technical, analytical and logical sequences, unless we have a particularly well-defined specialist interest. To make audiences sit up, we need to find a deeper connection.

You can technically be a good writer by learning to master phrases, vocabulary, grammar and syntax. You can be a decent emotional writer by seeking to move audiences by talking about things that *they* care about.

To reach the heights, though, you need to dig deep and pull out the grit and the conflict from the gut. That doesn't mean that your writing style needs to be angry or shouty. It can be very calm and very smooth. But if you reach down and find out what bothers you – deeply and personally – then you usually have something that cuts through.

What bothers you? Rubbish customer service? Expensive offices? Inefficiency? Poor product quality? Slow innovation? Excessive bureaucracy?

This isn't an invitation to scribble endless angry rants. You need to have solutions as well as questions. The best business leaders are the problem-solvers, finding answers to things that really bother them.

I think there's a good alignment between writing from the gut and leading a successful business. Leave the analysis and the flowery verse to others. Don't over-elaborate. Don't pull too much on the heartstrings. Just tell it straight, as you see it.

In a digital age – drowning in blogs, articles, posts, podcasts and videos – the authentic voices are the ones we look for. Who has got *something to say*? Not just cheap emotion or intellectual construct – who, out there, *feels something deeply*?

It goes back to the first principle in this book: BELIEF. With writing, don't worry too much about the technical skills. Instead, spend the time working out what you feel deep down.

The 'voice of the writer' is an overused and meaningless term. It's simply *your voice*. Discover it by finding something that stirs your belly. That's your route to authenticity.

Summary

- **Remember the five Ws:** Who, what, when, where and why. Whether it's a speech, an article or even an email, be clear about the actors, the scene and their motivation. To the five Ws, add another: how do we fix it? In business, you are first and foremost a problem-solver.

- **Rewrite everything to make it clearer:** The first draft will always need revision. Strip out long words. Shorten sentences and paragraphs. Make language visual and ask questions in your writing. Use groups of three, alliteration and (occasionally) rhyme. Repeat key points.

- **Write from a deeper place:** Work out what makes you passionate as a human being. Decide what you feel strongly about. To write well, you need to care about the subject and the material. If you do – and keep the language simple and conversational – that will be more important than any style guide.

CONCLUSION

I'd like to bring this book to a close by highlighting two stories which embody the core principles I have been discussing in PR for Humans:

Belief. Clarity. Opinion. Energy. Context. Time. Humility. Imagery.

I'll begin with a major news story from the beginning of my reporting career: the death of Princess Diana.

The People's Princess – London, 1997

1997 was quite a year. Tony Blair was elected by a landslide. Diana, Princess of Wales, was killed in a car crash in Paris. And I fell in love with Georgina, the woman who would become my wife and the mother to our two incredible sons.

I had my first paid job in journalism, as an assistant producer at APTV, a video news agency which supplied TV pictures to broadcasters all around the world. The shots and sequences we edited would ultimately be seen by billions of people, especially during a huge global story. There was no bigger headline than the death of Diana. In the first week of September 1997, the eyes of the world were on the UK, and on London.

As the managing director of APTV, Stephen Claypole, told us: this was the most significant event many of the most experienced journalists in the organisation had ever worked on. In his view, it was the biggest story many of us were ever likely to encounter. For Georgina and for me – the young guns in the APTV newsroom – it was certainly the first epoch-shifting moment of our fledgling careers. (Now, of course, we look back on others: 9/11, the invasion of Iraq, the financial crisis and Brexit.)

Tony Blair, then widely adored, had come out with his tribute to the 'People's Princess'. The country was in shock. The accident in Paris had come as a sudden blow to millions who adored Diana. There was genuine tragedy, particularly for the two young princes, William and Harry. But something else was going on. The media and the general population fell into a cyclonic embrace of emotion. To many people, journalists were the enemy. Plenty believed the paparazzi had chased Diana to her death. Journalists themselves became giddy with the swirling sentiment of the story – a story we were right at the centre of.

CNN and Sky News had for some years been running what was back then called 'rolling news', news which continued non-stop, 24 hours a day, sometimes to the ridicule of the snootier editors at the BBC and other, more established broadcasters. (In November of 1997, though, the BBC was to launch its own rolling News Channel, which continues to this day.) There was no Twitter back then. No Facebook. No Instagram. No smartphones. But, already, technology was accelerating. The speed of news was increasing. Journalists were no longer just reporting *on* the news – they were often part of it. They were feeding it. And it was feeding them. Events and reporters began spinning together, in a dizzying and often uncomfortable dance.

On the Tuesday evening after Diana's death, I was sent down to Buckingham Palace to talk to mourners and look at the growing heap of floral tributes. The pile of flowers was large, but the scenes were as you might expect, given the death of a significant national and international figure. As the week went on, however, events – and the reporting of events – developed into a feedback loop of extraordinary force. Audiences watched flowers being laid and emotions build. That triggered a deeper response. They went to lay more flowers. The scenes were broadcast back into living rooms. The intensity of the story multiplied by the day, until the hour of the funeral arrived. By then a vast field of flowers extended out from the gates of Buckingham Palace. The service itself – with Elton John's 'Candle in the Wind' and Earl Spencer's fervent address – seemed to blow the top off an emotionally bottled nation.

In the newsroom, some of the hard-bitten cynics occasionally still smirked and made light remarks, as is the way of journalists. But I remember feeling genuinely moved on that September day in 1997. I had a date with Georgina that evening. We managed to leave the newsroom at 6pm, well before the ratcheting news demands had begun to ease. It was our time. We had our own plot to figure out. And yet, that day we couldn't escape the news. We didn't know Diana personally. We didn't know any of the main actors. Yet we, along with millions of others, found it hard to walk out and just get on with other things.

The death of Diana was a story about BELIEF. Millions of people believed it was a meaningful moment, and therefore it was. There was CLARITY: it was about one person and one tragedy. Everyone had an OPINION about who was to blame and how others should respond. The whole nation was roused by emotional ENERGY. The CONTEXT – of a fresh new government, out-of-control tabloids and a monarchy adrift – was crucial. It was about the past. It was about change. It was about the future – the country Britain was becoming. It was about TIME. The Princess of Wales had empathy and HUMILITY in life. Her sons, William and Harry, provided the lasting IMAGERY, on a day of heavy symbolism. Two boys walking bravely behind their mother's coffin.

Belief. Clarity. Opinion. Energy. Context. Time. Humility. Imagery.

There's Power in Love – Windsor, 2018

Another royal day provides the bookend to this part of my story. It was a much happier occasion, in May 2018, when the boy who walked behind Diana's funeral cortege watched his bride walk up the aisle of St George's Chapel in Windsor. We'd seen Harry's story unfold over the intervening 21 years. The emotional struggles of his childhood. His youthful lapses of exuberance. His dangerous tours of duty in Afghanistan. His dedication to improving the lives of wounded servicemen and -women. Now his marriage – symbolising transatlantic diversity.

At these moments, those of us in the audience reflect on our own lives: the struggles, the dangers, the disappointments. The things we've gained. The things we've lost. Our lives as humans are played out in story. But it is only when watching the stories of others that we can allow ourselves to step back. Only then, sometimes, do we reflect on the arc of our own script. Only then might we dare to assess where we've been... and where we may end up.

On that sun-drenched day in May, the best of England was on display. It was a day of outrageous beauty. A day remembered for the performance of an American pastor. Michael Curry's wedding sermon was strange, long and meandering. But it sure was memorable.

"Two people fell in love and we all showed up... There's power in love. There's power in love to help and heal when nothing else can," said Curry, his eyes spinning, his hands gesticulating, his powerful, resonant voice unlike anything ever heard inside those ancient chapel walls. The speech was loaded with metaphor, with opinion and with passion. And, boy, was there energy:

> Imagine this tired old world where love is the way. When love is the way – unselfish, sacrificial, redemptive. When love is the way, then no child will go to bed hungry in this world ever again. When love is the way, we

will let justice roll down like a mighty stream and righteousness like an
ever-flowing brook.[39]

An electrifying – if to many observers, bizarre – sermon. Even the best
speeches can be improved by making a few cuts. Certainly, more clarity in the
message would have been good. And dear old Curry could have reflected the
context with a lot more precision.

As for time? Well, that principle went completely AWOL. But realising
he'd gone on way too long, Curry then improvised one of his best lines:

We gotta get y'all married!

The nervous prince, apparently blessed with his mother's humility and
empathy, sat nervously transfixed (or confused?) with his new bride. And, for
all of us watching, it felt like this was, even for just a day, an odd little piece
of our story too.

Human PR

In his speech, Michael Curry made a single solitary reference to the economy:

Imagine business and commerce where love is the way.

For many of those watching, this would have been stretching things a bit
far. Sure, talk about 'love' in the context of families, marriage, communities,
hope, injustice, politics... even war. But business and commerce? Really?

I haven't spoken much about love in this book. But I have spoken a lot
about stories. About people. About audiences. About humans.

To many, particularly in Britain, where heart-on-the-sleeve emotion
hasn't been a historical strength, even mentioning 'stories' in business feels
too soft. Too touchy-feely. Too light. Too insubstantial.

To those people I say, fine, go back to your spreadsheets, your cluttered
PowerPoint slides, your tangled presentations, your boring speeches – you
can keep them.

To those, however, who relish the power of words, those who look for
authentic leaders, those who want to be moved, I say, step this way. There's
a better, more powerful and ultimately more valuable way to approach the
craft. It's this: focus on the person and not the organisation. Find out who
they are, what they believe and how they might bring their story to life.
Find the emotional connection. If that person is you, if you are the leader or

---

[39] Michael Curry, royal wedding sermon: www.youtube.com/watch?v=fTMWJU9Nafk

CEO of the business, think about how you can use timeless principles to cut through and be remembered.

Belief. Clarity. Opinion. Energy. Context. Time. Humility. Imagery.

Don't imagine that communication is about 'strategy' and 'metrics' and 'measurable outputs' and 'grids' and 'stakeholder mapping'. When comms and marketing people talk about those things, say, OK, but what's the story, folks? How do we move an audience from one point to another? In a busy, noisy world, how can we reach people? How do we make this meaningful *for them*?

Tell a powerful story. By humans. For humans.

This is all PR has ever been. It's all PR will ever be.

If you've enjoyed what you've read in this book, or wonder how these ideas could be applied to your business, then please do contact me directly: mike@prforhumans.com

Thanks for reading!

Mike

SELECT BIBLIOGRAPHY

Anderson, Chris *TED Talks: The Official TED Guide to Public Speaking* (Headline Publishing: 2016)

Aristotle *Nicomachean Ethics* (Oxford University Press: 2009)

Aristotle *The Art of Rhetoric* (Penguin Classics: 1991)

Bailey, Stephen and Roger, Mavity *Life's a Pitch: How to Sell Yourself and Your Brilliant Ideas* (Corgi: 2008)

Blanchard, Paul *Fast PR: Give Yourself a Huge Media Boost* (Right Angles: 2017)

Botelho, Elena L., Powell, Kim R. and Raz, Tahl *The CEO Next Door: The 4 Behaviours that Transform Ordinary People Into World Class Leaders* (Virgin Books: 2018)

Browne, John *Connect: How Companies Succeed by Engaging Radically with Society* (WH Allen: 2016)

Campbell, Alastair *Winners: And How They Succeed* (Penguin Random House: 2015)

Carnegie, Dale *How to Win Friends and Influence People* (Vermilion: 2006)

Collins, Jim *Good to Great: Why Some Companies Make the Leap and Others Don't* (Random House Business: 2001)

Harari, Yuval Noah *Sapiens: A Brief History of Humankind* (Harper and Row: 2014)

Harris, Robert *Imperium, Lustrum, Dictator* (The Cicero Trilogy – Arrow: 2009–2016)

Heath, Chip and Heath, Dan *The Power of Moments: Why Certain Experiences Have Extraordinary Impact* (Bantam Press: 2017)

Hieatt, David *Do Purpose: Why Brands with a Purpose do Better and Matter More* (The Do Book Company: 2014)

Humes, James C. *Speak Like Churchill, Stand Like Lincoln: 21 Powerful Secrets of History's Greatest Speakers* (Prima Publishing: 2002)

Keller, Gary and Papsan, Jay *The One Thing: The Surprisingly Simple Truth Behind Extraordinary Results* (John Murray Learning: 2014)

Kermode, Robin *Speak So Your Audience Will Listen: 7 Steps to Confident and Authentic Public Speaking* (Pendle Publishing: 2013)

Lancaster, Simon *Speechwriting, The Expert Guide* (Robert Hale: 2010)

Leighton, Allan *On Leadership* (Random House Business: 2008)

Nadella, Satya *Hit Refresh: The Quest to Rediscover Microsoft's Soul* (William Collins: 2017)

Nihill, David *Do You Talk Funny? 7 Comedy Habits to Become a Better (and Funnier) Public Speaker* (Benbella Books: 2016)

Phillips, Robert *Trust Me, PR is Dead* (Unbound: 2015)

Plato *Republic* (Penguin Classics: 2007)

Sinek, Simon *Start with Why: How Great Leaders Inspire Everyone to Take Action* (Penguin: 2011)

Stanislavski, Konstantin *An Actor Prepares* (Bloomsbury Academic: 2013)

Merlin, Bella *The Complete Stanislavsky Toolkit* (Nick Hern Books: 2014)

Webb, Caroline *How to Have a Good Day: The Essential Toolkit for a Productive Day at Work and Beyond* (Macmillan: 2016)

Whitmore, Sir John *Coaching for Performance: The Principles and Practice of Coaching and Leadership*, 5th Edition (Nicholas Brealey Publishing: 2017)

Williams, Marcia *The Romans: Gods, Emperors and Dormice* (Walker Books: 2014)